John C. Pellew   N.A., A.W.S.

ACRYLIC LANDSCAPE PAINTING

Watson-Guptill Publications / New York

Published in the United States of America 1968
by Watson-Guptill Publications
165 West 46 Street, New York, New York
All rights reserved.
Printed in Japan.
Library of Congress Catalog Card Number: 68-27551

To Elsie with love

Contents

Preface

With John Pellew's experience, ability, and knowledge, he should have been writing books on art instruction long ago. But over the years he has been in such demand as an illustrator, art director, teacher, lecturer, fine art painter, worker in national art organizations, puppeteer, and paterfamilias that we can assume that book writing could have been achieved only by renouncing sleep. But he is still young — as artists are judged — so he has plenty of time to make *this* book simply the first of a successful series.

Authoring books on art is not a particularly remunerative endeavor. As Ernest Watson, of Watson-Guptill Publications, commented when he first invited me to write a book: "You'll never get rich from this kind of work, but you'll attain great and continuing satisfaction from the benefits conveyed to others." And Ernest ought to know — and does know — for few teachers have contributed more to the art training field and been more cordially blessed by students than he.

And from what does this satisfaction stem? Well, Cellini spoke for all creative workers when he suggested, in his famous autobiography, that anyone who has achieved standing in the world should be prepared to share his hard earned knowledge with others — as John Pellew does here. One quality that is characteristic of the truly great is humility, and as a result most leading creative workers instinctively strive to convey all they can to their upcoming successors while Father Time still withholds the scythe. I have never known a first class artist who would refuse to share with beginners all he had accumulated through years of observation, study, toil, and reflection. I know there are certain second-string painters who, jealous of their few "tricks," would never wield their brushes in the presence of others; but even they form a negligible minority. Great creators have always given freely to students and apprentices — given time that could bring greater material payment if devoted to additional production.

The creative mind is always busy and inquiry indicates that the urge is born with the possessor. John Pellew began remunerative work early. As a teenager, he was apprenticed to a firm of marine engineers, repairing British mine sweepers in the closing years of World War I, working out of Penzance in Cornwall, his native city. And from that unaesthetic start he progressed through various other occupations: commercial sign lettering, painting theatrical "murals" on frail-appearing scaffolds high above the sidewalks of New York's Times Square, and various others up to the really artistic ones mentioned in my first paragraph. John's obsession is art, and virtually all his waking moments are devoted to its production or contemplation.

With a mind so oriented, John is fortunate that he has Elsie at his side to handle the mundane matters while he scans Parnassus. Elbert Hubbard suggested that behind every accomplishment you'll find a woman — one who fostered the interest that made possible the achievement or nourished the body so that the spirit could soar. So no story of John's success would be complete without reference to Elsie, the other member of the team.

John and Elsie and my Eileen and I have worked together on many an art project. Each knows what the other can do. John, for instance, is a demon for experimentation — in oil, watercolor, casein, tempera, and acrylics. With the last-named medium, he has had unusual success. It is the newest of the "wonder" media — one whose possibilities have been only partly uncovered, because of that newness — though enough has been done to show that it can be used in the characteristic manner of any of the other four media just mentioned, and that many new uses are possible.

The universally known Famous Artists School, of Westport, Connecticut, came into being at about the same time that the weekly, *Colliers*, folded. So it was only natural that John Pellew should transfer his talents from the magazine, for which he served as art director, to the correspondence school.

For the past twelve years, he has been a member of the school faculty, giving personal instruction by mail to an average of five students a day. This is really quite an assignment, for each work submitted by the student must be analyzed and its faults corrected by means of marginal notes and sketches. A sizeable corrective detail painting is usually made for each student, after which an individual, comprehensive letter of explanation must be dictated. My mathematical wizardry shows me that, at five lessons a day, an instructor will have given out, in twelve years, more than twelve thousand such lessons — an imposing teaching career that is also reflected in John Pellew's book.

Westport is also the headquarters of the renowned Fairfield Watercolor Group, an aggregation of twelve nationally known illustrators, fine art painters, and their wives, who have met each month during the past eighteen years to analyze and criticize paintings made by individual members. This competition, among artists of such standing, has served for each as a remarkable, post-graduate art course — a course that could not fail to sharpen both the painting and analytical talents of all. John and Elsie Pellew, naturally, are members of the group.

Needless to say, a professional history as impressive as John Pellew's should qualify one to write a pretty good book on art instruction. I have a feeling that the readers of *Acrylic Landscape Painting* will go along with me on that thought.

Frederic Whitaker

Acrylic Landscape Painting

The Flight of the Gull Acrylic on Masonite, 20″ x 30″

I think this is a good example of what I've called an intelligent use of the camera. There was no time for painting when I visited this headland at Zennor in Cornwall. The day was bright and sunny, the sky clear, and the ocean pure ultramarine blue. The photograph, taken with color film, was so vivid in color that it was almost gaudy. I wanted to paint the scene; but to copy the photograph would have been disastrous. It would have been merely another tourist travel picture. The shapes were good and required little changing. I first made a black and white dry-brush drawing. The photograph was then put aside and not looked at again. I limited my palette to very few colors. If I remember correctly, they were yellow ochre, burnt umber, raw sienna, Mars black, and titanium white. The burnt umber produced warm grays, the Mars black cool ones. By completely changing the color scheme, I made the picture a dramatic statement, rather than the garish one that it *could* have been if I'd allowed the camera to dominate my thinking. Yes, the gull was there, but not in the position where I placed it when I designed the picture space.

Chapter 1

Why paint in acrylics?

Why paint in acrylics? Well, why not? I think the coming of this new medium is a definite breakthrough for the artist who is seriously interested in technical processes.

The tempera painters of the Italian Renaissance experienced such a breakthrough with the arrival from the north of a new medium called oil paint. This oil based paint made many things possible. One was the easy blending of edges. The tempera painters' tedious cross-hatching was no longer necessary. No doubt there were some diehards in those far off days who held the view that tempera was good enough for them and who held out against change of any kind. I've heard similar views expressed by contemporary painters about the new acrylics.

The advent of a new medium doesn't mean that the old will disappear entirely. Egg tempera is still being used — and being used magnificently by Andrew Wyeth, among others. I make no claim that acrylics are better than oils, traditional watercolor, or egg tempera. But I do say that this new medium is different and tremendously exciting. New avenues open up to be explored — avenues that can lead to technical effects not possible in other media. Acrylics present a challenge. Why not accept that challenge? I think *any* experience that teaches you something about the materials of the artist is worthwhile. I've always felt that the artist who specializes in one medium only is missing much of the fun of being an artist. I feel that painting is a craft and I'm convinced that the painter should know as much as possible about the many ways of painting a picture.

Adjusting to a new medium

We all know the watercolorist who scorns the use of any opaque pigment (such as white gouache) and insists that the right way to paint a watercolor is in transparent washes only, with the white of the paper being used to obtain the lights. This sort of artist is the so-called purist. Now, although I'd be the last to decry the beauty and charm of a good traditional watercolor (having painted hundreds myself) I do feel that such insistence on "rules" is limiting.

There's no one way to do anything. A serious study of the watercolor paintings of that great 19th century Englishman, J. M. W. Turner, reveals the fact that he was familiar with every possible use of the medium. Until the coming of acrylic, there was simply no way to do anything technically different or new in watercolor — no way that Turner hadn't discovered. He'd done it all more than a hundred years ago. He worked in transparent washes, in gouache, wet in wet, and in combinations of all three. He accepted no limitations. If acrylic had been invented in his time, I'm quite certain he would have given it a try

When they first use acrylics, many painters make the mistake of expecting it to be like the other media, but with the added convenience of fast drying. When they encounter difficulties, they blame the new medium, not themselves. Acrylic must be thought of as new — and anything new must be learned. "It is a medium to grow on," says Lawrence N. Jensen in his book, *Synthetic Painting Media*. It's a medium capable of a whole new range of effects. This is not to be taken to mean that the painter should change his *style* of work. The realist remains a realist; the nonobjective painter remains nonobjective. It merely means that the artist will discover new and intriguing effects that would not have been possible in the older media. I'll demonstrate and discuss some of these effects in later chapters.

What are acrylics?

But just what is this new medium?

All paints consist of three things: powdered *colors* (pigments) or dyes; a liquid *vehicle* that actually functions as a kind of "glue" that will make the color stick to the surface of canvas, paper, a panel, or a wall; and a *thinner* which the artist adds to the paint to make it the consistency he prefers.

With a few exceptions, the same pigments and dyes are used in all types of artists' paints. The real difference between paints is in the *vehicle* and the *thinner*. In oil paints, the vehicle or "glue" (mixed with the pigments or dyes by the manufacturer) is a vegetable oil called linseed oil; the thinner is a wood product called turpentine. In tempera, the vehicle is egg yolk, or whole egg, or even a mixture of egg, oil, and varnish — thinned with water. Watercolors are made with a water soluble glue called gum arabic, again thinned with water.

In these three traditional kinds of paint, the vehicles are all *natural* materials. In acrylic, the vehicle is *synthetic,* a manmade product of modern science. The acrylic vehicle is actually a liquid plastic, which performs the same function as linseed oil, egg, or gum arabic — but does it better in many ways. Thinned with ordinary tap water, the acrylic vehicle dries quickly to a tough, flexible film which won't crack and takes a lot more physical wear and tear than any other medium; once dry, acrylic paint is insoluble in water and tough as nails.

The manufacturer compounds acrylic artists' paints from most of the usual pigments and dyes (plus some interesting new ones) and acrylic emulsion (as the vehicle is called); the paint is packed in tubes, jars, or plastic squeeze bottles. The artist adds water as he needs it, or thins the paint with pure acrylic emulsion, which makes the paint creamier than water and produces excellent glazes. A variant of the emulsion is used to make acrylic varnish.

Rapid drying

The quick drying of acrylic paints seems to bother some painters. I've found this quality an advantage rather than a detriment.

Acrylic requires less than thirty minutes to become dry to the touch. This allows color glazes to be painted over opaque underpaintings the same day — even the same morning. I don't think the old masters, who waited months for underpaintings to dry before they could begin glazing, would have quarreled with this; they would have been delighted! The watercolorist will find that color washes set quickly, allowing a second wash to be painted over the first without fear of picking up the undertone. Quick drying also permits you to paint detail almost immediately over thick impasto — for instance, the masts and rigging of ships against the sky. This is a difficult task in wet oil paint. The painter must take this quick drying into consideration at the start and learn to use it to his advantage.

For years, artists have been warned of the danger of too early application of varnish on oil paintings. The advice of the experts has been to wait two, even three years. With acrylics, three hours is more than enough time! So much for the convenience of quick drying.

Acrylics compared with other media

I've already noted that acrylic is a *different* medium. Some additional comments may be in order concerning the specific differences between acrylic and other media.

Let's compare it first to oil. In what manner does acrylic differ? The oil painter who likes to work day after day into wet oil paint — taking advantage of the slow drying time so he can change his mind, scrape paint off, and do all sorts of subtle blending — will be troubled by the fast drying time of acrylics. When you paint in acrylics, you can't scrape off and start over if you change your mind, simply because the paint dries too fast; instead, you simply paint over the mistake. Actually, this is a great advantage, but it takes getting used to. Furthermore, because acrylic dries so quickly, you can't keep brushing the same passage until you get the subtle blending and transitions which are so dear to oil painters — in flesh tones and skies, for example. You *can* get the same kind of subtle transitions by using drybrush, scumbling and glazing, thus taking advantage of the quick drying time, rather than fighting it.

To some extent, the fast drying of acrylic can be retarded by adding gel to the paint; this is a colorless medium, described in Chapter 2, which gives the pigment a buttery consistency and imparts a glossy, wet look to the finished painting. Gel can be purchased in studio size tubes wherever acrylics are sold.

Many oil painters favor a rich, "fat" paint which they produce by adding stand oil, sun thickened linseed oil, and various varnishes to their oil paint. The resulting paint has a "tacky" feel when applied to canvas with a brush or knife. The oil painter who likes this tackiness will miss it when he tries acrylics. The newer medium can produce the same results — the same feeling of richness and gloss — but the *feel* of the paint is different. Acrylic is lean, like gouache or tempera, and therefore doesn't allow the brush to drag or stick in a thick, juicy, fatty paint surface.

However, a good craftsman can learn to give his acrylic paintings the same glowing appearance as his oils. In fact, if the proper varnish is used on a finished acrylic painting, it's impossible to tell whether oils or acrylics have been used. Once again, see Chapter 2, in which varnishes are discussed.

When acrylics are used in a traditional watercolor technique, thinned with water to a transparent consistency, the differences between acrylic and watercolor are not as great or disturbing as some painters may feel. The only really important difference is that an acrylic wash, once dry, cannot be washed out. This is obviously tough on the painter who keeps changing his mind and who arrives at the finished watercolor through a series of mistakes. However, there's no help for this man, whether he paints in acrylic or in watercolor; although acrylics may add to his frustration, he still won't paint a successful watercolor until he learns to get things right the first time.

I've been able to do everything with acrylics that I previously did with traditional watercolor. In fact, I take advantage of the fact that a dried acrylic wash is permanently set and can't be washed out. It's wonderful to superimpose wash over wash without fear of disturbing the color beneath. Some acrylic watercolorists take even greater advantage of this characteristic; a mistake can be painted out with white acrylic and a fresh wash applied just as if you're painting on clean paper. Most of my exhibited "watercolors" have been acrylics, in recent years. Unless they're told, viewers accept them as traditional watercolors.

In many ways, acrylic is vastly superior to tempera if a tempera technique appeals to you. I'm not a tempera painter by inclination, although I do one or two paintings in this technique each year. I succumb only when a subject really calls out for a tempera treatment. My first experiments were with traditional egg tempera; I tried both pure egg yolk with water and emulsions of egg and oil. If they're kept too long, even in the refrigerator, both smell to high heaven! Acrylic medium stays fresh and sweet and doesn't need refrigeration. Furthermore, egg tempera paintings often develop a web of fine cracks. I have yet to see an acrylic, painted in the tempera technique, crack.

I might conclude by pointing out that acrylic also beats oil paint as far as permanency is concerned. In oil paint, the danger of yellowing is always present. And the more oil is added, the greater the danger. Tests show that acrylics don't yellow with age and don't crack.

One set of paints for all techniques

What else? Well, for the student who has to consider the cost of materials, there's the obvious advantage of having one set of paints for all techniques. Out of the same box of tubes come watercolors, temperas, and paintings that resemble oils. The medium for thinning the paint comes out of the kitchen faucet — plain cold water.

I'm sure that I'm not alone in my dislike of the messy cleanup after a day of painting in oils: the sticky, dirty palette and brushes; the paint rags needed to clean them; more rags and turpentine needed to clean myself.

How different it is when acrylics are being used! The metal, plastic, or glass palette is simply flooded with water. In a few minutes, even the hardened paint can be removed with a razor blade or a palette knife. A rag or paper towel is used to finish the job and the palette is once more bright and clean. Brushes (kept wet throughout the painting day) are easily cleaned by washing in soap and water. The paint rags dry stiff and hard. They can be thrown away without fear of spontaneous combustion as they contain no flammable materials, such as oils or varnish. (Some people save them to make collages.)

All the paintings reproduced in this book were painted with acrylics, no matter how different they may look. The brands used were Liquitex (manufactured by Permanent Pigments), Aqua-Tec (produced by Bocour Artists Colors), and Hyplar (made by M. Grumbacher). Other good brands include New Masters, Shiva, the Mexican Politec, and the British Cryla (made by Rowney). I used the tube colors. Details concerning materials are given in the next chapter.

Cornwall Acrylic on Masonite, 21″ x 39″

The moorland of the Land's End district of England is the area that W. H. Hudson, the great nature writer, called "Cornwall's Connemara." This isn't an exact portrait of a definite place, but a composite of three different places which, when put together, create the character of the whole district — or so I feel. The big rock outcropping on the skyline is Carn Galva, which I climbed many times as a boy. The buildings seen against the sky are what's left above ground of one of the old tin mines, many of which dot the Cornish moors. Notice how the picture has been given depth by the use of cool color in the distant parts, a play of both warm and cool in the middle distance — the triangle of land below the mine — and warm color in the foreground. It's good to keep in mind that cool color appears to recede and warm color to advance. Note how the building sets the scale of the scene. The dark shapes in the foreground are patches of dead bracken and heather. This painting was awarded the thousand dollar Seley Award at New York's Salmagundi Club. Collection, Columbia University. Photo, Juley. Study the detail on the left.

The White Boat, Lanesville Acrylic on Upson board, 9″ x 12″

As landscape sketches go, I'd say that this one is fairly realistic. Yet if you blow up a section of it — say the area around the lobster boat — you'd find that the details are merely suggested and are not the least bit photographic. They're painted in a sort of shorthand, the type of treatment that every outdoor sketcher develops in his own way. This brings us to the question of what creates the illusion of reality. Most amateurs seem to think it's the careful painting of small details. This isn't true. This sketch contains no real detail. Yet it's realistic. Why? It's the correct relationship of the tonal values that creates the illusion of

reality. If the value relationship is correct, the most simply painted sketch can convey an impression of reality. The student must learn to "see" values. Here, for instance, the trees are dark against the sky, but not as dark as the shadowed side of the largest building. The front of this building is its lightest part, but not as light as the rock ledge below it. Look at something in nature and ask yourself if it's lighter or darker than something near it. Then ask *how much* lighter or darker. It's not only a matter of seeing; it's also a matter of thinking, comparing, judging.

Chapter 2

Materials and tools

Being a tidy person by nature, I keep my acrylic paints and brushes separate from those used for other media.

Sketch box

A 12″ x 16″ wooden sketch box serves the purpose quite well. There's ample room in it for a dozen tubes of paint, provided that I don't carry extra large studio size tubes. I can also fit in plenty of brushes, rags, and even a tin to be used for painting medium or water. The shallow, round tins in which you buy canned salmon or tuna are ideal; they're just the right depth to fit under the palette in the sketch box. This puts everything but water and the easel in one box — the importance of which I'll comment on at the end of this chapter.

Palette

What about the palette? The conventional wood one, sold with the wooden box, will have to be discarded. Acrylics stick to the porous surface and too much water warps the wood. This makes cleaning difficult. The right palette to use with acrylics must have a hard, smooth surface. A piece of white Formica makes a good palette for the paint box. A plumbing supply house or a large hardware firm is a likely source of supply for this material. Small pieces are often left over from counter installation jobs and the supplier will cut the size you need. With a hard surface, cleaning up becomes a pleasure instead of a chore (see Chapter 1).

The larger palette for work in the studio can be a sheet of glass. White milk glass is the best, or try a butcher's enamel tray. Both have a hard surface that's easily cleaned with water and a razor blade. Just soak dried paint in water and scrape lightly.

Brushes

And what about brushes? Here I imagine I'll raise a few eyebrows when I confess that I most often use *housepainters'* brushes for my larger acrylics — those larger than the small panels I carry outdoors. Some artists' brushes are used for finishing touches. The housepainters' brushes are made of nylon. They're cheap and they're easily cleaned. I started using them a few years ago, before nylon artists' brushes were available. Acrylics can be washed from nylon because of its slick surface. The traditional hog bristle or sable hair brushes are more difficult to clean; they're also expensive.

Artists' brushes of nylon are now on the market, of course. They're very good for acrylic painting, but they're still more expensive than my pet brushes purchased at the local hardware store and lumber yard.

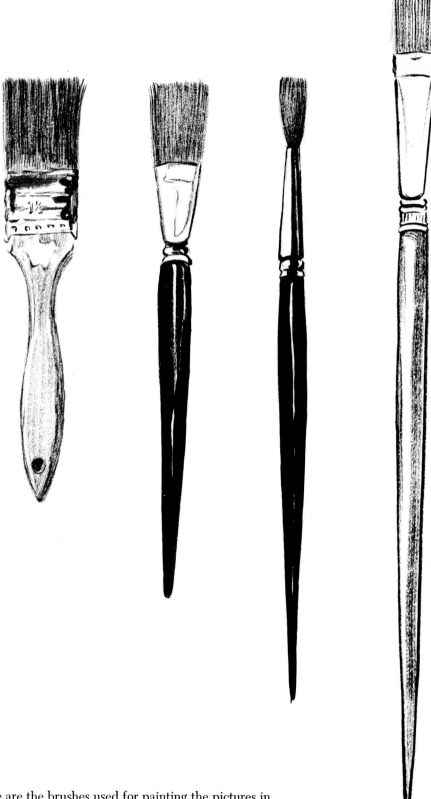

Here are the brushes used for painting the pictures in this book (left to right): 1½″ nylon housepainter's brush; 1″ oxhair flat watercolor brush; well worn No. 9 round sable; artist's flat nylon brush; small pointed sable for fine details.

Knives

In addition to brushes, acrylic can be applied with knives. You can use the same sort of palette knives and painting knives used for oil paint, although you ought to bear in mind that you have less time to push the paint around because acrylic dries so quickly. You must be very decisive about your knife strokes; just put them down and let them go.

To produce thicker paint suitable for palette knife painting, it's worthwhile to experiment with the acrylic "gel" medium, which I'll describe in a moment. To produce even thicker paint, you can buy a can of acrylic modeling paste. It's almost as thick as putty and mixes easily with acrylic colors from a tube or a jar.

To clean fast-drying acrylic off a knife, simply soak the knife in water for a while. If the paint doesn't peel off by itself, you can easily scrape it off with another knife or with a razor blade.

In addition to knives, you may want to try out a variety of tools that will scratch or texture wet paint. There are artists who use combs, dental tools, putty knives, etching needles, and all sorts of unorthodox implements.

Colors

Acrylic paint is sold in both jars and tubes. Some brands come in plastic squeeze bottles. The jar colors dry more rapidly. The tube color has the consistency of oils and takes a little longer to dry — but not much!

Guard against putting too much paint on the palette at one time. Skins start to form on some colors in twenty minutes. Some painters delay the drying by spraying the paint with water from a perfume atomizer. I haven't found this necessary.

I no longer use the jar colors. The tubes are a lot less trouble to transport. If the tops are kept tight, the paint remains moist and usable to the last drop. Tubes are essential for work in the field.

My pictures are all painted with what I suppose you'd call a limited palette, especially when I'm working outdoors. I work as simply and directly as possible, using the fewest colors I can get along with. What I mean by this is that I have nine colors in my box (plus white), but I use only four or five for any one picture. My complete list of acrylic colors is as follows.

(1) AZO yellow medium
(2) Yellow ochre
(3) Raw sienna
(4) Cadmium orange
(5) Cadmium red, light
(6) Burnt sienna
(7) Phthalocyanine blue
(8) Cerulean blue
(9) Burnt umber
(10) Titanium white

I carry no prepared greens. My greens are all mixtures of yellows and blues. The tenth tube in the box, titanium white, is used only when I paint in the opaque techniques. Let me tell you a bit more about each color.

AZO yellow medium is a brilliant yellow with which good transparent washes can be obtained. It is much less opaque than cadmium yellow, which I don't use. I use it for bright yellow greens, mixed with just a touch of phthalocyanine (thalo) blue. Another useful yellow of this type is Hansa yellow, said to surpass cadmium yellow in permanence.

Yellow ochre is a natural earth, a dull yellow or tan, with medium covering power, used by most landscape painters. (However, Claude Monet and other French Impressionists banned all earth colors from the palette.) I find yellow ochre useful in autumn landscapes. Mixed with burnt sienna, it produces beautiful warm tones. When painting acrylic watercolors, I often give the paper a pale wash of yellow ochre prior to painting.

Raw sienna is another earth color, actually an ochre containing silicic acid, and therefore darker than yellow ochre. I mix it with blues to obtain rich greens. Raw sienna is especially good for foliage when something darker and richer than a yellow green is required.

Cadmium orange is just what the name implies: a bright orange color. Like all the cadmiums, it is quite opaque. I sometimes use it to create colorful grays by mixing it with cerulean blue and white. This mixing should be done loosely on the palette, first dipping the brush into one color, then into another; too much mixing may result in a green tone. I use this mixture only in opaque painting.

Cadmium red, light. I seldom use this color in mixtures with other colors. I use it by itself where I need a really bright red note, one that really sings. But I avoid using it in mixtures.

Burnt sienna, when used transparently or as a glaze over a light toned underpainting, is a fiery, almost red orange. In landscapes, I use it in mixtures with thalo blue to obtain deep greens.

Phthalocyanine (thalo) blue is a good blue in all techniques, but one that can "take over" a picture if the artist isn't careful. It has extraordinary tinting strength. On the palette, it should be kept as far away from the light colors as possible. It makes a fine transparent wash for skies.

Cerulean blue is a heavy, dense pigment and will settle into the grain of watercolor paper, creating textural effects that are sometimes useful. In landscape, I often use it for cool tones in the distance.

Burnt umber is the only dark brown on my palette, most often used in opaque techniques, but also used in the watercolor technique, mixed with phthalocyanine blue to obtain grays. In opaque painting, I mix it with blue and white for grays. I also use burnt umber for toning a gesso panel and sometimes with white as an underpainting for oil colors.

Titanium white. Unless you grind your own colors, this is the only acrylic white presently on the market. It is a good white, with plenty of covering power. There should be no need to use any other.

Medium

Rather than thin acrylic paints with water, many painters prefer to extend their paints with acrylic medium of one kind or another. If you're using acrylic as a form of watercolor (see Chapter 5), water is the proper thinner. However, for other techniques, you may find one of the three basic types of acrylic mediums more suitable.

Gloss medium is simply the pure acrylic emulsion — the same adhesive liquid that the manufacturer mixes with pigment to make paint. You can buy the medium in a bottle and mix it with tube paint or paint that you spoon out of a jar. Whereas water actually makes the paint thinner, the medium produces a rather creamy consistency, something like oil paint thinned with linseed oil and varnish. Many painters prefer this creamy consistency because it's more "brushable" than paint that's simply thinned with water. The dried paint is shiny and luminous.

You can also buy matte medium in bottles. This is exactly the same as the gloss medium, but with some silica added to make the medium dry to a non-glossy finish. Like the gloss medium, the matte medium produces creamy, "brushable" paint which is more like oil paint than acrylic which is simply thinned with water.

The third acrylic medium is called gel and comes in a tube. It's thick and gummy and you mix it with your paint to produce a really thick consistency which comes out very much like oil paint. This medium is particularly helpful for palette knife painting and textural effects whenever you want knife or brush strokes to show strongly.

All of these mediums can be slightly thinned with water, although it doesn't pay to add a great deal of water because you then lose the advantage of the medium; you might just as well thin the paint with water and let it go at that. Some painters thin the gloss or matte medium half and half with water to produce a consistency which is more like milk than like cream.

Don't be put off by the rather opaque white appearance of the medium in the bottle. As soon as it dries, it's clear.

Painting surface

Acrylics will stick to any surface that's not greasy, oily, or non-porous. This gives the artist a remarkably wide choice of materials to paint on. Paper, untempered Masonite, wallboard, and linen are the ones most often used.

For watercolor technique, I use 300 lb. cold pressed watercolor paper. My advice here is to try the many papers available and then stick to the one that works best for you.

Masonite makes a fine rigid support. It's sold in 4' x 8' lengths. If you're unable to cut it up yourself, the lumber yard may oblige — for a small fee. The *untempered* variety of Masonite should be purchased; the *tempered* Masonite is impregnated with oil to toughen the surface, but in time this could prove damaging to pictures painted upon it. (Remember, acrylic won't adhere as well to an oily surface.) I use the ⅛" thick sheet. Sizes larger than 20" x 24" should be cradled, that is, glued to a wooden frame (see sketch). This is done to prevent warping. Smaller sizes shouldn't warp if both sides are coated when the gesso ground is being applied, as I'll describe in a moment.

Upson board, a trade name for a type of wallboard, can be used. This material is easily cut with a sharp mat knife and is much lighter in weight than Masonite. I recently found this board being manufactured with a canvas texture pressed into one side. This makes wonderful sketching panels for opaque painting.

Good Belgian linen is more expensive than the other materials, but when properly prepared with acrylic gesso it makes an excellent support for acrylics. Linen must be stretched on the conventional canvas stretcher.

Preparing the surface

Watercolor paper, of course, needs no preparation of any kind — just a short prayer before tackling its terrifying whiteness. The other supports must be prepared. They *can* be painted on directly without preparation, but then you sacrifice the traditional underlying white ground (which I feel is so essential).

I prepare untempered Masonite and wallboard in the same manner. First the smooth side of the Masonite (the side I paint on) is sanded with fine sandpaper (this isn't necessary on wallboard) and the dust is removed with a damp cloth. Acrylic gesso is then poured into a clean can and thinned slightly with water (the gesso, when you buy it, is rather thick). The gesso is applied with a nylon housepaint brush. The size of the brush I use depends on the size of the panel being covered. A 2″ brush is a handy size for most panels. After coating the surface, I turn the panel on end and coat the edges, sealing them. One coat is sufficient here.

When the gesso on the smooth side (the painting surface) has dried, I turn the panel over onto a clean sheet of newspaper and coat the back. This also receives only one coat. On reaching the damp (but not dry) stage, the panel is turned right side up and the smooth painting surface receives the second coat of gesso. This time no water is added. How many coats to use will depend on how thick the gesso is applied. Some painters use just one coat. I brush the gesso out well and apply three coats.

The preparation of wallboard is the same as for Masonite. The larger sizes of this material must also be cradled (fastened to a wooden frame) to prevent warping.

Linen need not be coated on both sides. First stretch the raw linen. When stretching, care should be taken not to pull or stretch too tight; the water in the gesso causes shrinkage of the linen which, if stretched too tight, may warp the stretcher. Gesso can be applied with a knife or a brush. The edge of the knife will force the gesso into the weave. This makes a good ground to paint upon. Again, the number of coats is up to the individual. When it looks and feels right — it *is* right.

Varnish

Any acrylic painted on a panel or on prepared canvas should be given a protective coat of varnish on completion. When acrylic is used as a watercolor on paper, the painting needn't be varnished, but it should be framed under glass like any watercolor.

There are two types of varnish: matte and glossy. The first dries with a satin-like sheen, the second with a high gloss. They're easily applied with a flat brush. A slight milkiness shows up as the varnish is painted on, but disappears on drying, when the varnish becomes clear as glass.

Whether you use the glossy varnish or the matte variety is just a matter of taste. The glossy kind makes your colors a bit more luminous and produces an effect somewhat like a well varnished old master. The matte varnish has no shine, of course, and therefore keeps your colors subtle and atmospheric. It all depends upon whether you like the satin finish that we associate with watercolor, pastel, or casein painting — or the glowing sheen of a well varnished oil. You can also try mixing the two varnishes to get a semi-gloss finish.

Yours truly going sketching.

Here's everything set up, all ready for work.

How much equipment?

How much or how little should you carry when you paint outdoors? This is a question that has bothered painters, both amateur and professional, for a long time. I think the amateur always carries too much. I've watched them in the summer art colonies, setting out to paint loaded like a camel in a desert caravan.

Now here's a sketch of yours truly going painting. Paint box in one hand

and an easel over my shoulder — that's all. There are three panels in the lid of the box and a flat (witch hazel) bottle full of water in my pocket. More equipment wouldn't make my painting any better or make the working procedure any more comfortable. The next drawing shows everything set up, ready for work.

Easel

Is an easel necessary? I think so. Some painters sit on the ground or on a low stool when they sketch outdoors. This makes quite an operation out of getting up and walking back to view the sketch from a distance. Brushes and other tools, spread at the painter's feet, are easily kicked into the grass or into a crack in the rocks and lost. I like to keep things off the ground; that's my reason for using an easel.

The one I use is called the Anderson or Gloucester easel. It will hold a small panel or a canvas as large as 30" x 40". It has no bolts or screws to get lost, it's quickly set up, and it's very sturdy. The so-called French combination box and easel is very popular, but a little complicated for my taste.

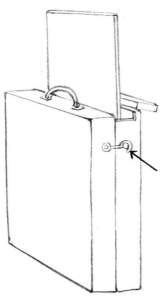

Here's how a 16" x 20" panel can be carried in a 12" x 16" box.

Some additional tips

I find a small bottle of 612 insect repellent a useful addition to the paint box during the summer months.

That's the extent of my outdoor equipment. *Everything* is in one box — an important consideration when you're climbing over coastal rocks or making your way through the woods. Of course, if larger pictures are to be painted, more water must be carried.

A 16" x 20" panel can be carried in a 12" x 16" box without adding any additional problems. It's done in this way. Simply slide the 16" end into the slots in the lid of the box, allowing the panel to extend beyond the top of the box. The hinged flap, of course, must be left open. To keep the box closed, attach hooks to its sides (see sketch).

My final word on what to carry is the same advice I give students on painting procedure. Keep it simple.

People on the Rocks Acrylic on Upson board, 11″ x 14″

In summer, the rocky shores of Cape Ann are dotted with what the New Englander calls summer folk. The bright colors of their clothing create interesting contrasts with the grays and browns of the rocks and the surrounding ocean. There were no people on the rocks the day I painted this sketch. However, as I worked, the memory of another day, when I had seen a painting class at work along the shore, came to mind. It was the work of a few minutes to paint in the little figures. What would have been just another rock sketch instantly became something much more interesting. The small spots of color added a gay note and the figures set the scale, giving a small picture the illusion of bigness. The figures were painted with a small pointed watercolor brush. With acrylic it was no problem. They went right over the rocks and sky, which were quite dry by the time I was ready for the figures. It would have been more difficult with oils. I first sketched the composition with a little burnt umber. The sky and ocean were the next to go in. Then came the rocks, and last of all the little people.

On a Hedge in Cornwall Acrylic on Masonite, 16″ x 20″

The hedges in Cornwall are really stone walls that have been taken over by nature since human hands first raised the stones. Lichens and soft cushions of moss decorate their surface. Ferns, gorse, and wild plants of all kinds grow upon the stones. Some of the hedges are very old, having stood for centuries. This picture is typical of a section of hedge in mid-summer: a tangle of wild flowers and lush green growth. The light gray tones in the center foreground show where the covering has been torn away, revealing the face of the granite rock beneath. I started this painting by laying in a variety of dark tones in the area that falls behind the flowers. I then worked upon the lichen covered rocks in the foreground and upper right. The little yellow flowers were painted over the dark background with pure titanium white which, when dry, was glazed with a thin wash of AZO yellow. The other blossoms were then positioned. My lay-in was now complete. All that was left to do was to paint the detail. I started at the top and worked toward the bottom. When I reached the lower right corner I added my signature and that was that. This picture is deceiving. There's not as much work here as one would suppose. It took two mornings, about 7½ hours to paint. However, I must point out that I worked every minute of those hours. Study the detail.

The Berkshire Hills Acrylic on watercolor paper, 15″ x 18″

This is a memory painting, not a portrait of a place. We've driven through the foothills of the Berkshires in Massachusetts many times. The memory of one early morning view from a motel window remained with me until I put it down on paper. I tried to capture the effect of morning just after sunrise. I think I pulled it off, but much of the effect depends on color, which is lost in black and white. My drawing was simply two light pencil lines: one along the top of the hills and another at their base. I first gave the entire paper a wash of a mixture of AZO yellow medium and yellow ochre. The clouds were put into this wet wash with a mixture of phthalocyanine blue toned down with a touch of burnt sienna. This was done rapidly to create a soft blending effect. The paper was then allowed to dry. Next came the warm tones of the hilltops — burnt sienna and phthalocyanine blue. The darker parts of the hills were painted with phthalocyanine blue toned down with burnt umber. The foreground was created with a variety of brushwork, including drybrush; the colors used here were yellow ochre, raw sienna, burnt umber, and burnt sienna.

Chapter 3

Getting used to the medium

Today, most books on the technique of painting have a chapter — or part of a chapter — on what is called technical exercises. These exercises are intended to teach the student how to hold and manipulate the brush and the knife, how to obtain different effects, and so on.

In my student days, we weren't taught exercises. We were taught first to draw: initially, from plaster casts and from still life; then from the model in the life class. If our progress was satisfactory, we graduated to the painting class. The little tricks of execution now known as exercises were supposed to come naturally as one's personal style developed. Thus, I'm afraid my training was inadequate, because I find today that my students do the so-called exercises better than I do!

If exercises bore you — as they do me — skip this part, and go on to the more interesting information toward the end of the chapter, where we deal with the actual painting of a picture. However, if you're totally unfamiliar with acrylic and you feel that it would be helpful to do some introductory exercises, here are some typical painting procedures for you to practice. If you've never handled acrylics before, doing these exercises will at least help you to get used to the medium.

Glazing and scumbling

One of the most important and valuable characteristics of acrylic is its remarkable suitability for glazing and scumbling. Because this new medium dries so quickly — and is waterproof when dry — you'll find that you can paint one transparent or semi-transparent layer of paint on top of another in rapid succession. This is a great advantage when using acrylic as watercolor (which I'll describe in Chapter 5), but it's also a great advantage in techniques that are more like oil painting.

For example, you may recall that the old masters often "mixed" their colors not by stirring them together on the palette, but by painting one transparent or semi-transparent layer over another like sheets of colored glass. They could produce a rich green by glazing a transparent coat of blue over a dry coat of yellow. Then they could tone it down by scumbling a semi-transparent haze of gray over the dried layers of blue and yellow. This sort of thing can go on indefinitely. Titian, for example, claimed that he could apply thirty or forty glazes and scumbles before he was through.

This is worth learning to do with acrylic. Try "mixing" your colors on the painting by applying various colors on your palette over one another in every combination you can think of. Try light colors over dark, dark colors over light, colors merely mixed with water, colors mixed with a bit of white to make them more opaque, etc. Among other things, you'll find that you can tone things down and make them move back in space by applying a semi-transparent glaze — which you can get simply by mixing a bit of white into any color you choose, but not enough white to make the color completely opaque.

The glossy and matte acrylic media are particularly useful in these techniques. Instead of mixing a glaze or a scumble with water, you can mix the paint with the medium, which makes it more brushable, but still just as transparent. (The medium is milky when wet, but dries completely clear.) A glaze or a scumble mixed with glossy medium will dry to a glowing, shiny finish, popular with the old masters. The same thing mixed with matte medium will dry to a duller, non-shiny finish which many modern painters favor.

In case you're not up on your old master techniques, perhaps I ought to define the words *glaze* and *scrumble*. A glaze is a transparent layer of color, usually applied over a dried layer of lighter color. A scumble, on the other hand, is usually a semi-transparent, light tone applied over a darker ground color. In both cases, the underlying tone comes through, but a glaze is like a clear sheet of colored glass while a scumble is like a cloudy sheet of colored glass.

Drybrush.

Drybrush

Drybrush is a technical device known to all workers in traditional watercolor. It is a wash of color laid with the brush skimming the surface of the paper, depositing color only on the ridges of the paper's irregular surface. Owing either to the rough texture of the paper, or to an exact estimate of the amount of pigment and water in the brush (which is kept fairly dry, rather than loaded) the color appears with innumerable gaps which allow the undertone to break through.

Drybrush can be used to advantage for many effects. Typical uses are the rough bark of some tree trunks, the variegated surface of a sandy shore, a weathered stone wall, or the sparkle of sunlight on distant water. Drybrush should be used with discretion and never overdone. A little goes a long way. The best results are obtained with a rapid stroke. Try the textures illustrated.

Graded wash.

Graded wash

The art of grading a transparent wash from dark to light is a process often done well by commercial artists, architects, and mechanical draughtsmen. It's useful for painting a clear sky blending from a fairly dark tone at the zenith to a light one at the horizon.

I find it best to wet the area first with clean water. Then, starting with plenty of paint at the top, I gradually add water as I progress toward the bottom with lighter and lighter strokes. This is probably the most difficult of all these exercises, but with patience and practice, it can be mastered; like riding a bicycle, once learned, it's never forgotten.

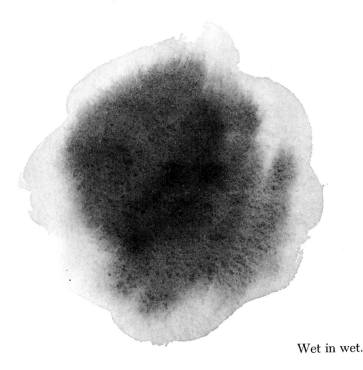

Wet in wet.

Wet in wet

Wet in wet is another watercolor technique that can be done easily with acrylics. It's especially good for soft, atmospheric effects, clouds, and fog. And it's simple to do. A brushful of color is put into a wet wash of another color and allowed to blend with it. It's a lot of fun, leading to many unexpected results and happy accidents — which explains its popularity with amateurs.

However, wet in wet effects are never used throughout the work by painters of the well planned picture. This is because the painter of the well planned picture never counts on — or even wants — an accident. He feels that he must be in control the whole time. What would be the use of planning a picture carefully if happy accidents are allowed to take over? The professional painter might use wet in wet effects in his sky or perhaps for some reflections in water, but all this is *planned*. It's not accidental. Even in pictures where I've used a great deal of wet in wet, I try to calculate the result ahead of time. However, if an accident does occur and turns out well, I say, "Thank you, Lord," and let it stay.

Palette knife textures

The same knife textures that can be executed with oils can be obtained with acrylics, used straight from the tube, or thickened with gel medium to a heavier consistency. I often use knife work when I'm painting masses of foliage. For instance, light can be applied effectively over dark. The point of the knife can be used to scratch lines into the wet paint, or thin lines of light or dark can be painted with its edge.

Acrylic has extraordinary textural possibilities. Although this new paint dries hard as a rock — and is therefore pretty hard to texture once it's dry — there are a great many things you can do with it while it's still wet. In

Palette knife textures.

addition to pushing it around and scraping it with the painting knife, painters have found that they can "comb" it with various texturing tools, press textured objects into the wet paint (like rough cloth) which leave interesting patterns when peeled away, and sprinkle anything from sand to metallic powder into the wet paint to give it additional tooth or sparkle.

If you mix your paint with gel medium, you'll find that the paint gets thicker and gummier, so you can try more experiments with textures. And if you really want to build up very thick textures, try the acrylic modeling paste, which is thick enough to make a bas-relief. The modeling paste comes in cans and can be scooped out with a palette knife and mixed with acrylic colors.

All these things are worth trying, but don't get carried away by gimmicks. Textures must have an expressive purpose and shouldn't become ends in themselves — as often happens with so-called palette knife painting. These textural effects should be used sparingly.

Painting in two transparent colors

All the usual brushwork done with watercolor and oil can be done with acrylics — plus some things that can be done with neither. Now let's paint a picture with this interesting new medium (see Demonstration 1).

I suggest that you do a simple subject in the transparent watercolor technique, using only *two colors*. This is a very limited palette, but much can be done with it, as you'll see. For the demonstration painting, I've chosen a harbor scene that's mostly sky and water, with some darker indications of boats and a wharf — a good subject for a simple statement, because it avoids a lot of complex detail. The colors to be used are burnt umber (a warm color) and phthalocyanine blue (a cool color). I suggest that you make your painting the same size as my original, which was a quarter sheet of watercolor paper, 11″ x 15″. Try a similar subject, but don't copy my painting, of course.

First sketch in the composition with an HB pencil. Next mix a pale wash of burnt umber, using plenty of water. Paint this over the *entire* picture surface. This is done to warm the cold white of the paper and to make it more receptive to the subsequent color washes. This first pale wash will serve to provide the lightest tones of the picture.

Now the cool middle tone of the clouds is put in. This is a mixture of the two colors, with more blue than umber in order to make the wash definitely cool in color. Try it out on a scrap of paper. If it's too light add more paint; if it's too dark, add water.

The next step is to add the dark cloud shapes, using burnt umber with only a touch of blue. I did this by rapidly twisting and turning the brush to obtain a ragged, wind-blown effect. The sky is now finished. I used a ¾″ flat brush throughout.

Now the distant land, the wharf, and the shore are put in with a wash of burnt umber. When this is dry, the distance is given an overwash of cool color.

Now the calligraphy of the foreground water and the middle tones of the wharf and the shore are developed. The final step is taken: suggesting the details that bring the picture to life — the boats, birds, figures, and the drying net hanging from the mast on the far side of the wharf. Incidentally, note the use of drybrush for the hanging net. The deepest darks of the wharf and shore are put in, and the picture is finished. The result of these consecutive steps, all taken at the proper time, is seen in the color reproduction, entitled *Down East*, on page 128.

The same subject could obviously be done in an opaque technique. However, with opaques, white paint (instead of water) would be used in mixtures with the blue and umber to obtain the necessary range of tonal values.

Other limited palettes

While acrylics are not difficult to use, I'd suggest working with only two or three colors at first. Quite colorful pictures can be painted with various combinations of a warm and a cool color. You may be surprised to find that brilliance in a painting is not arrived at by using brilliant colors; it's obtained by the juxtaposition of warm and cool colors and by strong contrasts of lights and darks.

A good three color landscape palette would be cobalt blue, yellow ochre, and red oxide. The yellow and blue mixed will give you interesting greens. The blue and red, mixed at full strength, create good dark tones. You won't get the exact colors you see in nature — but you wouldn't anyway, no matter how many colors you used.

Another combination that can result in deep, rich, colorful effects is cadmium red light, yellow ochre, and Mars black. A variety of warm and cool tones are obtained with mixtures of red and black. In watercolor technique, pale washes of Mars black look almost blue when they're placed next to a warm color. Yellow ochre mixed with red will produce orange tones; with black, yellow ochre creates fairly good greens.

In the next chapter, I'll deal at length with the use of acrylics in painting outdoors and in the studio.

North Country Drybrush on paper, 13″ x 18″

Drawn in New Brunswick, Canada, this cabin in its daisy strewn field, with the thick stand of second growth pines behind it, spells North Country. It was drawn on smooth two ply bristol board. The sky was left blank. I tried to suggest the band of white daisies along the base of the cabin.

Chapter 4

Outdoor and studio painting

Working in the field, face to face with nature, is a challenge — a gamble rather like hunting. Sometimes you bag something; sometimes you don't. It's exciting. Even now, after all these years, I'm still thrilled by early morning on a Cape Ann salt marsh or by October in the Connecticut woods.

For thirty years now, I've been painting outdoors, at first in oil, then in watercolor. After trying one, then the other, came a period of working in both, depending on the mood of the moment. But I now work outdoors in acrylic and find it an ideal sketching medium. In this chapter, I'll tell you why I feel it works well for me.

I'd worked some time with acrylics in the studio before trying them outdoors. My reason for sticking to the studio was that I believed acrylics would dry too rapidly in the open air. My painting experience *should* have told me that this would be an advantage rather than a disadvantage. However, one bright, sunny morning, feeling rather brave, I set up my gear on the marsh at the mouth of the Saugatuck River just below Westport. If I was ever going to make the test, this was the right kind of day to do it. No moisture in the air and a steady breeze off the land. My equipment was the gear I described in Chapter 2.

The importance of speed

Now if there's one thing that contributes most to making a successful sketch outdoors, it's the fact that speed is essential. Every professional knows this. Sunlight and shadow don't stand still. Getting that first impression down is the important thing. You must work at top speed, knowing that the very lighting effect that attracted you to paint a particular subject won't be there an hour later — may even disappear in ten minutes! I've never worked longer than an hour outdoors. On small panels, often less time.

I remember seeing an amateur painter in Rockport one morning, hard at work painting a street scene. Passing by four hours later, I found the same painter in the same place working on the same picture. Acrylics would have been no help to this painter. The fact that time is limited when working outdoors had simply not entered her mind.

My first outdoor experiment

Now let's get back to my breezy morning on the Saugatuck. Although I'll explain my opaque painting procedure in more detail in a later chapter, let me mention a few basic technical points. I started a 12″ x 16″ panel by first sketching in the composition with a brush and some burnt umber. The horizon line was placed well below the center of the picture area. (Most landscapes compose best with the horizon or eye level placed either below or above the center of the picture.) The flat marshland seemed to lend itself to a low horizon and a big sky. With a wash of burnt umber, I indicated a group of distant trees and followed this with a simple pattern of shapes for the land and water areas.

I then set my palette with white, yellow ochre, raw sienna, burnt sienna, and phthalocyanine blue. With the burnt umber already on the palette, this made five colors and white.

The foreground of my subject would soon be covered by the incoming tide, so that was painted first. I then worked on the sky with its rapidly moving clouds. Next, I added the grass areas and the water with sky and other reflections. Finally, the distant group of dark trees were put in and the sketch was finished. I worked for just under an hour and discovered that the quick drying acrylics had presented no problems of any kind. In fact, some of the colors I'd hardly used were just beginning to skin over; the lumps of color on my palette were starting to dry on the outside but were still wet within. I'd been working in the same technique I'd use in painting an oil sketch; I'd become so interested in my subject that, for a while, I actually forgot that I wasn't working in oil.

One thing I learned that morning was to give up my old habit of holding a fistful of wet brushes in my left hand while painting with the right. The soiled brushes, while not in use, had to be dropped into the water container to prevent them from drying out. Unless this is done, they become stiff with dry paint and can only be made usable again by some tedious work with a special cleaning agent. (Remember, acrylics are insoluble in water once the paint dries.) However, if they're kept wet while you work and cleaned with soap and water on returning to the studio, there's no problem. My procedure in the field is to rinse out the used brushes, then roll them in a paint rag before placing them in the paint box among the unused ones.

Another thing learned that morning happened unexpectedly. On taking the sketch from the easel, I fumbled — blame it on the breeze — and dropped it in the marsh grass *face down!* This would have ruined an oil sketch. But not the acrylic. In the short time it had taken me to put the brushes away, close the paint box and carry it a hundred yards to the car, my acrylic sketch had dried. When it fell, it wasn't scratched; nor was anything stuck to it. I'd discovered not only that I could handle acrylics outdoors, but that their quick drying was indeed an advantage.

Outdoor watercolor method

So far I've described an opaque painting procedure. What about the transparent watercolor approach? I'll describe this in detail in the next chapter. Here, I'll just mention that it's essentially the same as any opaque procedure, except that watercolor paper takes the place of the gesso panel and soft hair brushes are substituted for the stiffer bristle brushes. I seldom use more than three brushes: a ¾″ flat, a No. 8 round, and a small, well pointed brush for final details such as tree branches, etc. These brushes are all oxhair. I lack the courage needed to put an expensive sable brush into acrylic. I'm afraid I might forget to wash it out and wreck the brush.

A piece of 300 lb. cold pressed watercolor paper, fastened at the corners with masking tape to a 12″ x 16″ Masonite panel, is used as a support. This panel is taken from the lid of the paint box and placed upright on the easel. Painting a watercolor with paper in a vertical position may seem unorthodox, but hundreds have watched my demonstrations and they know it can be done. Of course, I paint directly on the dry paper, never using the wet method outdoors. On a so-called watercolor easel, the paper would be placed in an almost flat position; this often allows the sun to shine directly on the white paper, making it very difficult to judge tonal values. With the board upright on an oil painter's easel, the easel can be turned to the left or to the right, putting the paper in the shade. I've become so accustomed to this way of working that I'd find it difficult to work in any other way.

I find acrylics very easy to manage in the traditional transparent manner outdoors. My painting procedure is the same as I'd use with regular watercolor. If the subject is a straight landscape, a few marks with the brush and some diluted umber or ochre serve to indicate the composition. The sky is then painted as simply and directly as possible, followed by the middle distance, and finishing with the foreground, which is given only enough detail to suggest reality.

Size of outdoor paintings

What's the best size of paper or panel to use with acrylics in the field? That's a personal choice. I'd suggest any size that you and your equipment can handle in comfort. However, let me give you the benefit of my own experience. In oil, I've painted all sizes from 8″ x 10″ panels to 30″ x 40″ canvases. In watercolor, I've painted in every size from ⅛″ sheet to the full 22″ x 30″ sheet. Now I use only the smaller sizes outdoors. My panels for opaque painting are 9″ x 12″ and 12″ x 16″. For watercolor technique, I use the 11″ x 15″ quarter sheet.

Some of the best watercolors I've ever seen were small papers dashed off at top speed, the so called "quickie." I have several of my own that I wouldn't part with for anything.

Among the greatest landscapes ever painted on the spot are the small oil on paper sketches of John Constable, the 19th century English landscape painter. These tiny pictures (measuring, in some cases, no more than 7″ x 9″) are gems of the landscape art.

I think there are good reasons for using smaller papers and panels outdoors. They're convenient to carry. They take less time to complete and less time to dry. Acrylic sketches can be stacked one on top of the other because the paint is dry as soon as the water has evaporated. On an extended painting trip, there's nothing more exasperating than a batch of sticky, half dry oil sketches.

Some of my small sketches serve as inspiration for larger studio paintings. Some find their way into frames and mats — and eventually find an owner. Some go into the fireplace. A few I keep.

Studio methods

Painting in the studio — where there are comfortable surroundings and time for contemplation — presents no problems as far as size is concerned.

However, I'd warn the inexperienced reader against trying too large a size, too soon, for his first experiments with acrylics.

Stand or sit at the easel, according to your health, age, or inclination. I *stand* at a glass topped drawing table when I'm painting in watercolor; my palette, brushes, tubes of color, sponge, rags, etc., are on another table beside my right hand. For opaques and the tempera technique, I *sit* at an easel with a low table holding the materials at hand level on my right. Any small table with the legs cut down will serve. I use one that I built myself.

In the studio, I work mostly from small color sketches made outdoors. I sometimes work from drawings and occasionally from photographs. I find working from a drawing the most stimulating. Here I'm forced to put my visual memory to work in order to recall tones and color. The drybrush drawing reproduced on page 46 is an example of the kind of drawing I make to paint from. This drawing was made on two ply bristol board with waterproof drawing ink. I worked with a couple of old, rather well worn watercolor brushes. The picture painted in the studio from this drawing is reproduced on page 47.

When you're painting from a small color sketch, remember that although the medium is the same (acrylic) the larger work can never be merely an enlargement of the small sketch. An area that was simply suggested in the sketch — with a deft stroke or two — must now be given greater detail or a richer variety of textures. Acrylic lends itself to palette knife work and all manner of rich textures can be obtained. For textures, I use the acrylic unthinned, just as it comes from the tube. The larger the picture, the larger the knife used.

Used intelligently, the camera can be a useful tool. Many contemporary painters make use of photographs, although they seem reluctant to admit it. It is a known fact that Degas used them. Vuillard was an enthusiastic amateur photographer who made use of his photographs of friends and family. A recent biography of Paul Gauguin reproduced photographs he worked from. The English painter Walter Sickert was another. On the other hand, these great artists never allowed the camera to *dominate* their thinking. There's no point in doing something the camera can do as well or better. A skillful copy of a photograph proves only that the painter is a skillful copyist, nothing more.

I take photographs only if the locale is one that does not permit setting up an easel (such as a busy city street) or if I want a record of some detail that might be forgotten. In the studio, I make a black and white drawing from the photograph. The photograph is then put away and I work from the *drawing*. This assures me of a result that I hope is more artistic than photographic. After all, it's the personal style of the artist that makes a painting interesting, not how well a given scene has been reproduced.

In the next chapter, I deal with acrylic as I use it for the traditional, transparent watercolor technique.

The Felled Tree Drybrush on paper, 14″ x 18″

This beautiful tulip tree was struck by lightning and had to be taken down. Note the interesting shapes and textures. For the light gray tones, the brush was almost completely dry; rubbing it on the smooth paper created the desired tone.

Mahogany Island Drybrush on paper, 14″ x 19″

This drawing of rocks and trees was first sketched lightly in pencil. For the inking, I used some old watercolor brushes, wiping them out on the side of my drawing board to obtain the right degree of dryness in the brushes.

North Country Acrylic on watercolor paper, 20″ x 28″

This studio painting was made from a drybrush drawing made on Mahogany Island, St. John, New Brunswick. Elsie and I went to the island with a friend from the Audubon Society; she went to assist in banding the young seabirds, and I went to sketch. It's an interesting place, with rocky beaches strewn with driftwood, dense thickets, and windblown pines. This painting started as an experiment, a wish to try something I hadn't done before. I wondered what would happen if the watercolor paper were given a thin coat of acrylic gesso prior to painting. It seemed a shame to do this to perfectly good 300 lb. paper, but I was curious. It would be a different kind of surface to work upon. It was worth a try. I sketched the composition with a small brush, using acrylic burnt umber, merely a few guide lines for the composition. When the lines were dry, I applied the gesso, using one coat thin enough for the drawing to show through. This was allowed to dry. I then painted the picture. I found the thin gesso ground ideal for drybrush, which can be seen among the trees and in the vegetation above the rocks. My limited palette consisted of only three colors: raw sienna, burnt umber, and phthalocyanine blue.

Miss Pepys Acrylic on smooth paper, 11″ x 14″

She was named for the diarist Samuel Pepys. It wasn't until her first trip to the vet that we found she couldn't be called Mr. Pepys by any stretch of the imagination. This is a sepia, or to be exact, a burnt umber drawing on white paper. Although there's a little drybrush on parts of the animal's fur, this has been handled more like watercolor than the more typical drybrush drawings included in this book. The other drawings were intended as studies to be used for reference in developing a painting. Here I had no such intention. This is a complete statement. I think it says all I have to say about my friend Pepys. After rapidly sketching the composition with a well pointed HB pencil, I used Nos. 4 and 8 soft hair watercolor brushes. Because the cat was asleep on the bed, it was necessary to wake her once or twice to get the head raised. The pose would be held for perhaps a minute; then the eyes would close and the head would drop. Working on quite smooth paper is an interesting experience. I used two ply bristol for this drawing.

48

Chapter 5

Acrylic as transparent watercolor

The advice given in this chapter — on the use of acrylic as transparent watercolor — will be essentially the same as the recommendations given in any good treatise on watercolor technique (see Demonstration 2). Naturally, there will be some differences, but not as many as you may think. After all, a wash of color is a wash of color; if it's painted on white paper, it looks pretty much the same, whether you use pigment with an acrylic binder, or a gum arabic binder, as in watercolor. It's when a wash is painted over another wash, however, that the difference is revealed.

Retaining luminosity

The best watercolors are painted as simply and directly as possible. The essence of their charm lies in the luminosity and the freshness of the washes. To superimpose a wash over another is a tricky business, requiring skill and experience.

As far as the actual manipulation of paint is concerned, the oil painter has an easier time of it — I remind you here that I also paint in oil — because he can fight with his canvas, scrape out, overpaint, even recompose as he works. This, of course, is impossible with watercolor if spontaneity and freshness are to be retained. These essential qualities are most often lost when the painter tries to change a tonal value, or a color, by superimposing a wash over one that has already dried. If the underwash is not quite dry — or if the painter is heavy handed, too slow, or uses a brush that's too small — the result is a muddy mess and should be discarded immediately.

Now one of the special things about using acrylics as transparent watercolor is the fact that washes can be superimposed, one over the other, *without* picking up the underwash. Although this is good, you must also keep in mind that too many superimposed washes can deaden the picture's freshness and luminosity, even when you use acrylics.

What is the secret of this luminosity which I insist should be retained at all costs — this quality so highly prized by the purists who work only in transparent washes? It's obtained by allowing the white paper to gleam through all but a few final darks. This respect for the white paper is just as important when working in acrylics as it is when using the more traditional watercolor medium. The white paper is the very life of a good transparent watercolor. Winslow Homer's watercolors of Florida and the Bahamas are great examples of watercolors that make marvelous use of the white paper.

The tendency among amateurs is to overwork when they use watercolor. The way to overcome this is to cultivate a respect for the paper. Respect, not fear. This is important if the ultimate goal is to be a trans-

A World Full of Wonder Acrylic on watercolor paper, 20″ x 28″

This picture demonstrates that compositional rules can sometimes be broken, such as the one that tells us never to divide the picture space through its center. I did here; the tree and field areas are almost equal, and it doesn't bother me a bit. The figure of the little boy — my grandson, Jon, with what he called his duck spear — is balanced by the large black tree trunk on the right. Because of this, plus the feeling of a little figure in a big place, we're not conscious of the fact that a compositional rule has been broken. (Of course, now that I've pointed it out, you *will* be aware of the broken rule.) This is New England in October,

when the foliage color is at its best. Notice the bold, simple treatment of the trees and their dark values, contrasting with the lighter values of the field. Plenty of paint must be picked up on the brush to obtain good darks that retain a certain luminosity. Going over parts that have dried too light — in order to darken them — often leads to dullness, even in acrylics. Note the spatter and drybrush in the foreground, used to suggest detail and textural interest. These technical devices shouldn't be overdone. Study the detail of this painting on the left.

parent watercolor. One must guard against overworking. Nothing destroys luminosity more quickly than this regrettable tendency to add more and more unneccessary detail. Always remember that a simple rendering, with correct tonal value relationships, can suggest an illusion of reality far better than an overworked, finicky approach that tries to compete with the camera.

Paper

The best paper for transparent acrylics is good 300 lb. watercolor paper. Expensive, I know. The 140 lb. paper is cheaper, but must be stretched to prevent buckling. This is a nuisance. My advice to the beginner in acrylics, especially the outdoor sketcher, is to buy a full sheet of 300 lb. cold pressed watercolor paper (22″ x 30″) and cut it into quarters (11″ x 15″). This really gives you eight painting surfaces, because both sides are usable. Many of my best transparent jobs have been painted on the back of the paper — after a not so good attempt on the other side.

Some papers contain so much sizing (the glue-like substance that holds the fibers together) that it's difficult to make the first washes "take." B this I mean that the wash of color forms an area of bubbles, rather than a uniform tone. Such papers can be made more receptive to the color washes by first sponging the surface with clean water.

Brushes

The problem of what kind or what size brush to use — for suggesting the immense variety of detail found in nature — is one that seems to bother the amateur painter a great deal. How often, when doing a demonstration, have I answered the question, "What size brush are you using now, Mr. Pellew?" I may have been using a No. 10, but I could easily have done the same thing with a No. 8. The size of the brush (or what it's made of) isn't that important. If an artist has something to say, it *will* be said — no matter how meagre or magnificent his brush collection.

You needn't use sable brushes for watercolor technique in acrylic. In fact, it's better not to. Nylon and oxhair brushes are not only much less expensive, but easier to clean. "Use the largest brush you can handle with comfort" is the advice I always give my students. A great deal can be done with a ¾″ flat brush. Fully loaded with water and pigment, it will produce a large, flat wash. Held in a more vertical position, its edge can be used to create a variety of strokes.

Four or five brushes are all that you'll need for any acrylic watercolor. In fact, I seldom use more than three. In addition to the ¾″ flat, a couple of round brushes (a No. 9 and a No. 6) will be good choices. For studio painting on a full sheet of paper (22″ x 30″), a larger flat, such as the 1½″ size, will be handy; here's where you can use the nylon house-painters' brushes.

Drawing board

Whether you work with your paper in an upright position, or in a flat position, is entirely up to you. In Chapter 4, I described how and why I

The Great Arch Acrylic on watercolor paper, 22″ x 30″

This picture started with a pencil drawing in a small sketchbook. This was my usual procedure in doing New York street scenes. Next came a small watercolor, 7½″ x 11″, painted from the sketch. I liked it, framed it, and hung it in my living room for ten years. It was a visiting painter friend who induced me to attempt the larger version. It's not just an enlargement of the smaller picture. After all, ten years had gone by. I'd changed and so had my work. The actual scene had also changed; in fact, it no longer existed. The site is now occupied by a new office building. Anyway, I feel that I captured the mood of the original, but improved on the handling. It's limited in color: just burnt umber and phthalocyanine blue, with the white of the paper used for the lights. Except for the smaller details (the figures, etc.) it was painted with a 2″ nylon housepainter's brush. A No. 5 pointed ox-hair watercolor brush was used for the small touches. This painting was exhibited at The Metropolitan Museum's 200 Years of American Watercolor exhibition in December, 1966.

On the Beach Acrylic on watercolor paper, 15″ x 11″

I've heard it said that this subject has been done to death. Well, I suppose it *has* been painted a lot since Wyeth painted his famous dory in the field. But that's no reason for not doing it again, provided that it really moves you and inspires you to paint — and not because some artist you admire greatly has done it. If you're honest and paint it in your own personal style, without thinking of how someone else would do it, the result will be yours, as personal as your handwriting. I found this poor old broken boat alongside the rocks near the mouth of the Saugatuck River. I liked the strong top light on its deck and the tall weeds in the foreground. This picture was painted in watercolor technique. All but a few of the darkest darks are transparent washes. Some drybrush can be seen where the weeds overlap the boat, and also on the boat itself. There was no preliminary pencil work. The drawing was done directly with the brush. I worked from light to dark, with the darkest tones going in last.

work in the field with the paper in a vertical position. But when you're working with big washes of acrylic in the studio, I recommend a flat (or nearly flat) position. A large, upright paper can prove pretty discouraging to the beginner in acrylics.

I fasten my paper (300 lb.) to a drawing board by taping the corners with masking tape. Resting on a drawing table, the board can be lifted from the table and tilted this way or that way to prevent a wash from running in the wrong direction. This is a good reason for not fastening the paper to the drawing table. Tables are heavy to lift.

Painting technique

Most of my acrylic watercolors are painted directly on the dry paper, starting with the lightest tones and finishing with the darkest darks. I try not to superimpose too many washes, but aim for a bold, simple abstract pattern, then add only enough detail to suggest reality. Fussy detail is never necessary if the tonal values are correctly related.

I sometimes feel that a subject needs the wet watercolor treatment. The paper is then soaked in the bathtub for ten minutes, lifted out, and the water allowed to drain off via the corner. My drawing table is now covered with a sheet of glass and the wet paper is placed upon it. The surface water is blotted up and the paper is flattened with a clean towel. The nonabsorbent glass will prevent the paper from drying out too rapidly. However, don't delay. The time is shorter than you think. (If you can't get along without some pencil drawing, it should be done before the paper goes into the bathtub, since you can't draw on soaking wet paper.)

Working on wet paper, you must remember to pick up *plenty* of paint on your brush. This is especially true of the darks which, even in acrylics, dry out lighter in value than they appear when wet. The purpose in working on wet paper is to obtain soft, blended effects. As the paper dries, more definite brushstrokes and drybrush can be added.

However, if drybrush is overdone, much of the charm of wet watercolor is lost. Lucky indeed is the watercolorist who knows when to stop! Once a student learns to create a good drybrush texture, the tendency is to overdo this technique. Its overuse destroys the limpid charm of good watercolor. Drybrush can be used sparingly to render foliage, to suggest foreground details, and to create texture on the walls and sparkle on distant water — but *never* in the sky, where it's completely out of character.

Corrections

When traditional transparent watercolors are used, corrections can be made by sponging out, or by using a stiff bristle brush to scrub out unwanted areas. But acrylics are waterproof when dry and they're not as easily corrected, except in the opaque techniques.

Small sections can be lightened with a hard eraser. Be sure the paper is bone dry before trying this. Another way is to paint out the unwanted area with acrylic white, allow it to dry, then paint over it. The white must be smoothly applied if the patch isn't to show.

Above Hell Gate Acrylic on watercolor paper, 15″ x 20″

I lived for many years in New York City, beside that part of the East River called Hell Gate, on the Long Island side. There was a lot of good painting up and down the river. I explored every foot of the river bank from the 59th Street bridge to Bowery Bay, where the LaGuardia airport now stands. Like Sam Weller's knowledge of London, my knowledge of that part of the river was "both extensive and peculiar." This half sheet was painted from a sketchbook drawing, made on a cold, windy day, looking up the river to the Consolidated Edison plant. I used that plant, with its tall chimneys, in many of my early New York paintings. This one is in transparent technique throughout. I carefully saved the white paper for the patches of snow. The sky was painted wet in wet. Mixtures of phthalocyanine blue and burnt umber were painted into a pale, wet wash of yellow ochre and allowed to blend. The smoke was put in while the paper was quite damp in order to obtain a soft edge. I used the traditional method of working from light to dark, with the darkest darks going in last.

The Man from Folly Cove Acrylic on watercolor paper, 20″ x 28″

Notice what an important contribution the figure makes to the success of this painting. Without it, the picture lacks scale, depth, and, yes, even interest. Small figures often play a key part in landscape. They're seldom well done by the amateur. It's mostly a matter of drawing. Get the proportions and the gesture correct — forget the details. Don't paint features, feet, or fingers, the three f's. This is an autumn picture. The bushes at the right are in warm color: burnt sienna, raw sienna, and burnt umber. There's quite a bit of drybrush in evidence here. It was done with a flat ¾″ nylon brush. The rock area was first given a wash of yellow ochre, toned with a touch of burnt sienna. This was followed with darker tones made with mixtures of phthalocyanine blue and burnt umber. In the foreground, there's some calligraphy suggesting small stones or pebbles. This was done with my fingernail while the paint was still damp. The figure, of course, went in last over the sky, which was quite dry, having been the first thing painted. Colors on the figure are warm browns, except the trousers, phthalocyanine blue toned down with a touch of burnt umber.

Summer on the Avenue Acrylic on watercolor paper, 15″ x 16″

During the years when I lived in New York City, I painted hundreds of street scenes, of which this is typical. The paintings were all done from pencil sketches made on the spot. The beauty of working from brief notations, jotted down rapidly in a sketchbook, is that you retain only the vivid impression; so much is conveniently forgotten — so much unimportant clutter that would only do your picture harm if you remember it! The scene is Fifth Avenue near Central Park, just above 59th Street, on a summer afternoon. The handling is strictly transparent throughout, no white paint being used. A few light pencil lines, to establish the perspective of the sidewalk and park wall, was all the drawing done prior to painting. Like most of my transparent watercolors, it was worked from light to dark. The foliage was all painted before the trunks and branches were added. The greens of the foliage were obtained with mixtures of AZO yellow, raw sienna and phthalocyanine blue. I never know where the figures are going until everything else is done; then I place them where they'll work best as part of the picture's over-all design. The paper used was 300 lb. Capri. Study the detail of this painting on the left.

A Cat Called Boots Acrylic on watercolor paper, 20″ x 28″

You don't have to find a picturesque scene or a beautiful view to make a picture. Rembrandt painted a side of beef and created a masterpiece. Subject matter is where you find it — and I found this in the back yard. The open door of the garage, the stone wall, and some snow patches looked intriguing one morning in early spring. However, I needed a focal point in the composition and just at the right moment, before I could get the old pail and the tools I'd been thinking of, my focal point arrived and sat down. Boots, bless him, provided the picture's darkest dark and lightest light. He didn't stick around for long, so I put him in later, working from a pencil sketch. The picture would not be nearly as interesting without Boots. (He's gone now and we missed him for a long time.) This is the first acrylic I ever painted. It's seven or eight years old and hasn't changed a bit in that time. Don't think you have to go far afield to find good subjects. I firmly believe that the painter paints best what he knows best. Look around you. There's a masterpiece under your nose if you'll only see it. Collection, Elsie Pellew.

Behind the Dunes Acrylic on watercolor paper, 20″ x 28″

I'm sure that painting a picture with one brush is nothing important to boast about. However, this *is* a one brush painting. On arriving at the dunes and opening the paintbox, I found that all the brushes but one, a flat 1″, had been left at home. Luckily, the subject to be painted could be handled in a bold, simple manner; in fact it would be best to use that approach. My 1″ brush was just the brush for the job. When the picture was finished, I was glad the brush was the only one in the box. It forced me to take my own advice. I've often advised students to "use the largest brush you can handle with comfort." I was lucky that day on Wingaersheek dunes. The light toned sand in the sun is so white that it almost looks like snow. In contrast, the bushes, grass, and weeds along its top appear almost deep purple in their shadowed parts. From the foreground to the base of the dune, the color is quite warm. Because it was late September, the grass of the marsh had turned a beautiful warm ochre and the bushes in the right foreground were a deep warm brown, intermingled with the reds of poison ivy!

Below the Cliff Acrylic on watercolor paper, 20″ x 28″

This is one of the few full sheets that turned out as well as the small sketch it was painted from. The original was a quarter sheet watercolor. I liked it so well that I decided to try it in acrylic on a large scale. I was lucky; experiments of this kind often fail. The big rocky cliff is at Clodgy, St. Ives, Cornwall. It has been a favorite place with marine painters for a long time, both British and American. The big Atlantic rollers can be spectacular here. The little figures are artists' wives, waiting for their husbands to finish painting. I'd gone down to the beach to paint the ocean, but when I turned and saw the figures with their spots of brilliant color, dwarfed by the huge rocks, I forgot the surf. This was my kind of picture! The cliffs are painted in browns and blue grays. The nearest figure is wearing a scarlet scarf around her head and a black sweater. The other is wearing a bright blue sweater with a white collar. The flesh tones are a warm tan. The light, sandy beach is a mixture of yellow ochre with a little white. The patterns on the sand are burnt sienna and burnt umber. Notice the large, swiftly painted drybrush stroke in the right foreground. Study the detail on the left.

Wet Sunday Acrylic on watercolor paper, 15″ x 20″

There was a time, a few years back, when all the watercolor painters were painting rainy days. This one of mine was from a pencil sketch made on the river front in Astoria, on the upper part of New York's East River. I've walked along here so often, I could paint it from memory. What attracted me on this dreary, wet evening was the strong light reflected from the sky in the pools of rainwater, and the way in which the light made a silver arrow of the river. In order to give these lights dramatic impact, I made the dark tones around them darker than they actually were in nature. The sky was painted wet in wet after first wetting the area with clean water. Notice how its softness contrasts with the sharp edges in the foreground. The upper parts of the trees were first painted with some dark washes, put in at the same time the sky was painted. When this was dry enough, some drybrush textures were added, and then the dark trunks and branches. I painted around the figure of the girl because I wanted to do her raincoat in a transparent wash that had some luminosity. Sorry, but her legs are opaque. Study the detail on the left.

The Great Rock Acrylic on watercolor paper, 20″ x 27″

Here's another of my moorland pictures. As an experiment, I used a fairly smooth paper after soaking it for ten minutes in the bathtub. I suppose this could be called a wet watercolor, although much of the work toward the end was done when the paper had almost dried. The sky, with the suggestion of a distant shower, was the first thing to be painted and was put in while the paper was quite wet. The lighter tones of the distance, middle distance, and foreground came next. Because the paper was still fairly wet, these tones blended together and there were no definite darks or sharp edges at this point. The next step

was the big rock. The paper was now dry enough to keep the darks from spreading into the sky. I painted the whole shape with the middle tone, and immediately lifted out the lights by using the flat edge of a razor blade. The foreground was then strengthened and the dark tone along the horizon was put in. Last came the darkest darks on the rock and in the foreground. Note that there are few sharp edges; the paper was still damp enough to keep them soft. Some drybrush and spotting finished the picture, which was painted with two brushes: a No. 9 round oxhair and a 1″ flat. Study the detail of this painting on the left.

Deep Snow Acrylic on Masonite, 20″ x 24″

We who live in New England are privileged to view the constant panorama of the changing seasons, each one completely different from the next. What a wealth of material there is for the artist in this relatively small corner of the United States. Even the little patch of woodland seen from my studio window has several changes of costume during the year. I'm never tired of painting it. In fact, if need be, I could find a life's work here, the changes from one season to another are so great. In wintertime, the rolling hills and small farms of New England, with their covering of snow,

have a great appeal for painters. In this picture, I've tried to convey the feeling of fresh snow under a still overcast sky. There's light and shade, but no cast shadows. A great deal of paint was used in the snow in order to create textures. Note the scumble and drybrush type of treatment in the branches and twigs of the tree mass. Notice how the space has been designed to lead the eye to the small figure. The barns and the man's shirt are warm in color; the rest is mainly cool, with the exception of the sky, which is rather a warm gray.

Chapter 6

Opaque technique

If I were asked to name my favorite way of painting — transparent or opaque — I'd have to answer "both." For months at a time, I think that transparent watercolor is the most beautiful medium ever invented. Then I can become just as enthusiastic about painting a series of large canvases in oil and not go near a sheet of watercolor paper for an equal length of time.

I suppose my watercolors are best known because I've exhibited for so many years with the American Watercolor Society and the National Academy where I'm labeled an "Aquarellist" member. If the Aquarellist sends an oil to the annual exhibition of the Academy, he forfeits his exhibiting privilege and the work must go before the jury. So members working in both media seldom step out of the class (whether watercolor or oil) to which they're elected. I tried it once and was promptly put in my place. There was a large D for doubtful on the back of my canvas — which hung in the corner of a poorly lighted hall, at the foot of a stairway near a door labeled "Gentlemen."

So in the eyes of many I'm a watercolorist. But I'd rather be known as a *painter,* not as a specialist in any one medium.

This chapter deals with the opaque use of acrylics (see Demonstration 3). The opaque application of paint is the technique of the oil painters. This manner of painting can be duplicated easily with acrylics on canvas or on panels, with thick or thin paint, using a palette knife or brushes.

Toned gesso ground

Let's consider the first step: toning the gesso ground. As the painting is to be opaque and white paint will be used, there's no need to make use of the whiteness of the gesso ground as we'd make use of the white paper in a transparent watercolor approach.

I tone my canvases and panels with a gray obtained by mixing a little burnt umber with some titanium white. This is applied to the surface with a flat 2″ nylon housepainter's brush. The mixture should be about as thick as light cream.

Why tone the surface prior to painting? There are two good reasons.

First, it's easier to judge tonal values on a gray surface than it is on a white one. Placed directly on a white surface, a dark note looks so very dark that the inexperienced painter hastens to *change* it. However, when it's no longer surrounded by the brilliant white of the gesso, the dark note may look just right and may be weakened by the change. Of course, a gray toned ground is no *guarantee* that good value relationships will result; but it will help.

The other reason is that pure gesso is such a glaring white when you're painting outdoors, it's much more comfortable — easier on the eyes — to work on a toned ground. You needn't use a gray tone. Some painters like a buff or brownish yellow color. Others prefer a fairly dark reddish brown such as burnt sienna. Even a green ground might prove useful — perhaps for a painting of a summer wood interior.

Sketching the composition

I always sketch in my composition on the canvas or panel with a brush and burnt umber. There's no good reason for using this particular color, just habit. Any dark paint will do.

If the subject is a landscape, I first indicate the horizon or eye level, placing it well above or well below the center of the picture space. I might add here that I seldom compose a landscape in a vertical or upright shape unless a street scene is the subject. We're accustomed to viewing landscape (in nature) as a horizonal. Besides, let's face it, upright pictures don't *sell* as well as horizontal ones.

Now, still using burnt umber, I put down a few guidelines to establish the main elements and to create a well balanced design. At this stage the surface of my panel or canvas might look something like this.

First I put down a few guidelines.

The big pattern

The next step is the big pattern. Every landscape — even the most realistic — should be based on a good abstract pattern of dark and light shapes. This monochrome pattern of tonal values can be painted with the same burnt umber you use in sketching composition. It should never be more than a simple flat pattern: a plan for a picture, not a picture in itself. Details must *not* be thought of at this stage. The composition would now look like this.

Then comes the big pattern of tonal values.

Pattern is really another word for composition. The big, flat pattern which I begin with is not thought of as an underpainting — an underlayer of form or color that shines through in the final painting — but will be completely covered with opaque color in the next stage. It's merely a plan, a design for the picture space. In other words, it's a way of separating the job of composing from the final job of applying color.

This plan or pattern (or whatever you care to call it) is sketched in with a flat nylon brush. The size of the brush depends on the size of the picture. Except for a few final details — for which I use a pointed water-color (soft hair) brush — nylon brushes are used throughout.

Because of the quick drying properties of acrylic, these big masses can be established in broad, flat tones with no fear of a wet layer picking up an earlier layer of color.

While you're setting the palette with the colors to be used in completing the painting, this monochrome layin will dry and be ready to paint over. This approach clearly demonstrates one advantage of acrylic over oil. With oil, this underpainting would remain wet and work up into the superimposed color — unless you waited several days for the first layer to dry. For the student who feels the need to establish the composition in monochrome before thinking of color, acrylic is ideal for this purpose. Once applied, it's there, it's dry, and it won't rub out.

What makes a good landscape composition? A good pattern or composition in landscape has unity, balance, what painters call "oneness." If there's a rule that should never be broken, it's this: *don't try to say too much on one canvas.* If the scene contains more than one point of interest, you must ruthlessly suppress it so the one thing you have to say can be said strongly. Don't gossip in paint, as Robert Henri was fond of saying. Every year, I see student pictures that are quite well painted but contain enough material for three or four compositions — good ones — if painted on four separate canvases.

Rock Study Acrylic on Upson board, 12″ x 16″

This is a sketch, a study, something to be used later. I paint many of them outdoors. They're never exhibited, never sold. They're fun to paint and they help me store up a lot of information about nature. This one was painted at Andrew's Point, Cape Ann, on a day that was *not* what I'd call a good painting day. The day was too clear, the light too bright, and the sun glaring. I prefer some moisture in the air or more dramatic lighting. Anyway, there were rocks, sea, and sky — all good material — and something to be learned from painting them. (I've never painted the typical marine — the breaking wave with the rock to right or left — what my friend Harrison Cady called the white plume school; I leave that to the specialists.) I think I can see where this sketch of mine might turn into a picture someday, perhaps with foreground, some figures on the rocks, or a passing lobsterman and a flight of gulls. I'll think about it.

A genius can break the rules and get away with it. However, the student should guard against certain common flaws, like dividing the picture space through its center with the horizon line; almost all landscapes compose best in a horizontal shape, with more sky than land or more land than sky — never with an equal division. Don't place your dominant note in the exact center of your space; but don't let it hug the extreme edge either.

When all's said and done, composition is a matter of taste. If you think you don't have it, cultivate your compositional sense by studying the masters in the museums, in reproductions, or in art books.

Final painting procedure

Once I've established the big pattern, I usually start a landscape by painting the sky. This should not be taken as an indication that I work from light to dark. In my opaque acrylics, I work as I would with oils; at some time during the early stages, I decide where my darkest dark is going to be and put it in. I try to keep my other darks lighter in value than this one really dark tone.

I have no formula, no standard procedure, for painting a landscape. Outdoors, I see an effect of lighting and try to capture it as swiftly as possible. Working at top speed, I often forget the rules. In fact, I forget everything except the sketch being worked upon.

How do I know when I'm finished? Well, when I start reaching for a small brush to put in details, I'm finished. A few details, merely suggested, should be enough. Don't count windows.

I use the paint as it comes from the tube, only now and then dipping the brush in water, and then mainly to clean it. When working outdoors, I use no medium. There's enough in the paint, provided it's not thinned with too much water.

To varnish or not to varnish the finished picture, that is the question. Here, I think it's every man for himself. Some like a glossy finish, some like it matte. I do think one of these two types of varnish should be used to protect the surface. I lean toward the matte varnish. It brings out the tonal values without leaving a disturbing shine.

Applying paint

Now let's consider paint application — how thin or thick to use your paint.

I'm a thick paint man myself. Oh, I know that a masterpiece can be painted either way, but I love the feel of thick, juicy paint on a knife or brush. Putting it down, pushing it around, or painting into it can be sheer delight. My advice to students is to use plenty of paint. The manufacturer won't stop producing it. There's always more to be had.

Acrylics can be used impasto. If you like rich, buttery paint, gel can be added as I've said earlier. I seldom use it when working on small panels outdoors, but it might help the newcomer to acrylics. It does change the character of the paint somewhat, making it more like oil.

When a painter speaks of paint quality, he means the manner in which the paint is applied. Paint can be put on canvas in many ways: tenderly, brutally, sensually, or just plain ugly. There are good artists who have never developed a feeling for paint quality. The surface of their pictures shows the evidence of many changes of mind, with smooth and rough passages, thick and thin paint, that give the surface an unpleasant appearance. The work of these painters often looks best in reproduction.

Above all, good surface quality has unity — a feeling that the paint is a "fabric" whose quality is consistent throughout. This is true even with thick paint, where every brush stroke shows, as in the painted surfaces of Claude Monet or John Singer Sargent. To create this kind of surface when you work with acrylics, pick up plenty of paint on the brush and try to maintain the same thickness throughout. Don't paint thinly in some areas and thickly in others.

The theory of thin paint in the shadows and thick paint in the lights is a holdover from the old masters, good if you want to experiment in their techniques (see Chapter 9). However, the Impressionists never followed this "rule" and it's certainly no use to contemporary landscape painters.

I seldom make use of palette knife textures on small outdoor sketches. When I do use it, I do so *throughout* the entire sketch in order to create the same textural quality over the entire surface. I dislike a painting that has lumpy palette knife work combined with thin, smooth brushwork. The surface, as well as the composition, should have unity.

Light over dark

Painting light over dark is less of a problem with acrylics than it is with oil. This is particularly true of outdoor painting, where the oil painter is forced to work wet in wet. The worker in acrylic can wait a short time for the paint to set — or busy himself on some other part of the picture — then paint light over dark without fear of picking up the underpainting. A scumble, where a light tone is dragged or thinly painted over a dark in a manner that allows the dark undertone to show through, can be quite interesting. For instance, it suggests an easy way to create the texture of old boards or the bark of a tree. A thin, very fluid scumble is also a fine way to paint a fog or mist over darker objects.

The scumble does for the opaque painter what drybrush does for the watercolorist. But a word of warning. Never go overboard for a technical trick. There's nothing worse than a watercolor that's been drybrushed to death or an opaque painting that's scumbled all over.

Final details

As I've pointed out in Chapter 1, painting final details is an easy task with acrylics. In landscapes, I keep details to a minimum. The few that I use are usually the last things to be painted. Although the picture has been painted with thick paint, by the time I'm ready to add the details, the thick paint is dry enough to be painted over.

Such things as tree branches, telephone poles, or ships' masts against a light sky are no great problem. This is equally true of putting windows in a building. Any area that requires the painting of small detail over thick paint is easy with acrylic; but the under-layer would be very wet indeed if oil rather than acrylic was being used.

A Bright Morning Acrylic on Upson board, 12″ x 16″

Landscapes compose best with more sky than land or more land than sky. I keep repeating this to my students, but I sometimes break the rule myself. It's not a bad rule though, and it's worth keeping in mind. This painting is an example of the low horizon approach. It was painted from some high ground looking toward Rockport. An old instructor of mine once told me that a good composition was a dark picture with some light spots or a light picture with some dark spots. That's simplifying things somewhat, but there's some truth to it. I guess this painting would fall into the second category. The large dark mass is the base or foundation that once held a huge derrick, used to hoist blocks of Rockport granite aboard the boats. The water is out of sight. I needed a balance for this dark note, so I pulled in a bush that actually was quite a bit more to the right. Never hesitate to take liberties with nature if your composition can be improved.

Morning Fog Acrylic on Upson board, 9″ x 12″

I wonder how many pictures have been painted of Rockport Harbor on Cape Ann? Thousands probably. After all, the famous Motif Number One is there. I've painted there in all kinds of weather and expect to do so again. This small, quick sketch was made on an October morning when the fog was pretty thick. The color is quite limited, due to the enveloping gray mist. The palette was yellow ochre, raw sienna, burnt sienna, burnt umber, phthalocyanine blue, and white. The panel had been prepared with acrylic gesso and toned light gray. There are no real darks in the picture — none at all beyond the fish houses on the right.

Notice how the tonal values lighten toward the horizon. This is most clearly seen in the boats. The foreground boat has the most detail, while the distant boats almost disappear in the fog. In the foreground beach, there's a scumble of dark tone over a lighter undertone. This simply suggests the rough, pebbly texture of the beach. I used a couple of small, flat nylon brushes, and a No. 1 pointed watercolor brush for a few details, such as the boats, masts, etc. Knowing that the fog would lift (which it did), I completed the sketch in half an hour. Study the detail of this painting on the left.

Morning at the Met Acrylic on Upson board, 19″ x 20″

Museums have always proved a happy hunting ground whenever I feel the need for a change of subject matter. All of my museum pictures have either been painted from pencil sketches done on the spot or from memory, as this one was. I have enjoyed doing them all. I'm a people watcher, as well as a picture looker, when I'm in a museum. Young girls, portly old gentlemen, and the garden club matrons are all worth a rapid pencil sketch. A bald headed man, asleep on a bench below an old master, was once a happy discovery. *Morning at the Met* is a quick impression from memory. The interior, including the paintings on the walls, were all painted before the figures were added. However, I did have their position in the composition in mind right from the start. I often paint an almost square picture. I get tired of the so-called oblong standard sizes.

The Mandarin Jacket Acrylic on Upson board, 12″ x 16″

I'm sorry this isn't in color. The yellows and reds of the jacket, the white and pink hat, the greens and yellows of the sunlit grass, with the cool shadows cast by the trees, create quite a rich color harmony. I think the relaxed pose of the model has a lot to do with the appeal of this picture. I first sketched the figure on tracing paper and moved it around on the panel until I found where I wanted to place it. I then traced it in position and went over the pencil lines with some diluted black acrylic, using a small pointed watercolor brush. The spotting of the lights and darks is a kind of abstract pattern, arranged in a way that balances the figure and keeps the composition from being too heavy on one side. The whole of the picture is quite heavily painted. There's some palette knife work in the background trees and grass areas.

House Above the Beach Acrylic on Upson board, 12″ x 16″

This sketch, painted at Folly Cove, Cape Ann, in mid-September, shows that the palette knife can be used to good effect with acrylics. The palette knife is a useful tool, but should be used with discretion. It can be deadly in the hands of a mannerist who covers the picture surface with cute little gobs of paint that say: "Look at how clever I am! I did it with a knife!" It should be used as a means to an end and not as an end in itself. Walking down to the cove one morning, looking for a subject, I saw this house with its surrounding trees. I passed it by. It had no appeal for me. Going on to the beach, I painted the sketch that later

became *The Man from Folly Cove*. After resting and doing a bit of beachcombing among the rocks, I packed up my gear and started up the beach, heading for the highway. On coming to the house, I found that the lighting had changed; what three hours before was quite commonplace, was now a subject to delight the heart and eyes of a John Constable! It just had to be painted before the light changed; I thought the palette knife would be the quickest way to do it. The moral here: what may be nothing under one light can be a beauty under another. Keep your eyes open. Study the detail of this painting on the left.

Behind the Harbor Acrylic on Upson board, 9″ x 12″

When turned upside down, a good composition should hold together as a design. This small painting, when turned wrong side up, has the appearance of reflections in a pond. It's a good idea to view a picture this way at times. It gives you a fresh look at the composition, and errors in design are immediately apparent. This is a kind of all-over pattern of lights, darks, warm and cool color. The small boat near the center was made the picture's darkest dark, to act as a focal point. This, along with the contrast of the dark foliage overlapping the sunlit white house, keeps the eye of the viewer from wandering out at the sides. I won't pretend that this was all planned in advance. It wasn't. The experienced outdoor painter works these things out as he goes along. The foreground grass and weeds are quite warm in their fall coloring. The distant trees, being mostly in shadow, are cool in color. This color change creates an illusion of depth or recession; it might have been a rather flat picture if the warm to cool color scheme hadn't been used. Remember warm color appears to advance, cool color to recede. Study the detail of this on the right.

Improvisation Acrylic on watercolor paper, 20″ x 28″

Once in a great while (not too often, thank goodness) I feel the urge to paint something not based on realism. I haven't exhibited any of these experiments, but some of my fellow artists have found them interesting, so I include one here. I'm at a loss to describe it. Perhaps I should call it a series of controlled accidents. Strong colors were painted here and there on the paper, which was then placed on the grass outside the studio door and a stream of water from the garden hose played upon it. This was repeated two or three time. What's now the upper part didn't please me, so

I painted opaque white over it, creating some rather nice silver tones and textures of drybrush. Then came a lot of splashing and splattering, throwing paint spots from an old watercolor brush. The final touches were the dark blue squiggles along the foreground. I had no subject matter in mind, though most people see a subject of some sort. If you want to read something into it, go ahead. After it was matted, I found it rather interesting. Perhaps I'll do another some day. Is this any way to paint a picture? Study the detail of this painting on the left.

Inner Harbor in Fog Acrylic on Upson board, 9″ x 12″

Painting fog is the study of close values. The layman thinks it's difficult to do. Actually, it's much easier than painting the effects of sunlight and shadow. A fog scene has but few values and these few are much less difficult to relate than the many contrasting lights, darks, and halftones of a sunny day. Although the tonal values are close in this sketch, there *is* a feeling of recession. Notice how much lighter the distant buildings are than the building at the left. Notice also that the water in the foreground is darker than the sky. The strong top light on the wet road, along the top of the wharf, was a blessing; the picture wouldn't be as interesting without it. This light streak served to silhouette the cars and figures. The color is all warm and cool grays. Burnt umber, burnt sienna, phthalo-cyanine blue, and white were the only colors used. This was a very quick impression, taking about fifteen minutes to do.

86

October Salt Marsh, Maine Acrylic on watercolor paper, 9″ x 12³/₄″

This started out to be in watercolor technique. That's why it's on paper. However, the weather changed while I was working. A squall came up, creating a great dramatic sky and changing the color and values of the land completely. I decided it was too good to miss and went to work to capture the mood as quickly as possible. I discarded my transparent watercolor approach and worked with thick, opaque pigment, using both brush and knife. The trees were put in with the palette knife, then worked over with the brush. The warm colors of the maples, among the deep (almost black) greens of the pines and firs, with the strip of almost white sky above them, were very exciting. The autumn marsh grass took on a color that was pure copper. To capture effects like this — effects that come and go as this one did — it's necessary to work at top speed. The landscape painter should train himself to work fast. Nature doesn't stand still. The light changes; clouds appear or disappear; the fishing boat you're painting casts off; it starts to rain. Anything can happen. Get those brushes moving. It's later than you think.

Harvest in Cornwall Acrylic on Upson board, 19″ x 20″

A sentimental attachment to a place — or to anything else — is *not* a good reason for painting it. However, I just couldn't resist doing this one. It's based on an old photograph of my Uncle Dick Mann with his horses on my grandfather's farm near Land's End, Cornwall. I'd guess the time to be about 1888–89. Dick and the horses often posed for artists who had come to live and paint in Newlyn, which was a famous art colony at the turn of the century. The leader, if not the founder, of what art historians refer to as the Newlyn School was Stanhope Forbes, R.A., who settled there in 1881. Paintings of Uncle Dick and the horses by Forbes and others can be seen in many English art museums. I first made a pencil drawing of the horses and men on tracing paper. This was placed on the Upson board panel and held in place with two small pieces of masking tape. A second piece of tracing paper was rubbed with soft pencil (to make a kind of carbon paper) and put under the first. The drawing was then traced and the papers removed. Using a small pointed watercolor brush and some black acrylic, thinned with water, I went over the drawing. The sky was the first part of the picture to be painted, then the land areas, starting with the distance and working toward the foreground. The figures came next and finally the horses; I always save the most difficult part until last. The colors used were AZO yellow, yellow ochre, raw sienna, burnt sienna, alizarin crimson, cerulean blue, phthalocyanine blue, burnt umber, and white. Study the detail of this painting on the left.

Late October Acrylic on watercolor paper, 20″ x 28″

A favorite of mine is the small figure in a large landscape composition. There are many old fields of this kind in the vicinity of my home. What once was cultivated land is slowly being taken over by nature or by the building developer. But this particular field will always belong to nature lovers; it's part of a tract donated to the town of Westport for use as a Youth Museum. Its fields and surrounding woods have provided me with many good subjects. Students should look for two things in this acrylic watercolor: first, the soft blending of the wet tones of the trees in the upper part of the picture; then the superimposed calligraphy, suggesting details without becoming too realistic. I first soaked the paper until it was wet clear through. Placing it on the glass top of my drawing table, I blotted up the excess water and started the painting by floating washes of yellow ochre and burnt

sienna over the surface. Next came the dark mass of trees, for which I used raw sienna, burnt sienna, and burnt umber. Some of these darker tones (with a little more water added) were then painted along the middle distance at the base of the trees, and in the foreground. The paper was then ready for the final step, the touches that transform it from an abstraction to realism. Up to this point, I'd used large flat brushes. The foreground weeds were now rapidly painted with a round oxhair watercolor brush. A few dark tree trunks — and some fingernail scratches to suggest light ones — went into the trees, and the paper was then allowed to dry. Then the figure was painted, taking care not to overdo the detail. The very last things to be done were some opaque touches to suggest small wild flowers among the weeds in the foreground and the bright red leaves in the upper left.

Chapter 7

Mixing transparent and opaque techniques

Most of my watercolors, as well as my acrylics in watercolor technique, are actually combinations of transparent and opaque (see Demonstration 4). This does not necessarily mean that opaque white paint is used. Once sufficient paint has been picked up on the brush and put down thickly enough to prevent the white paper from gleaming through — that area is opaque. The strength of the American school of contemporary watercolor lies in this willingness to depart from conventional standards, to paint not only transparent or opaque watercolors, but pictures that actually combine both methods.

The importance of experimentation

Experimentation is in the air. A few years ago, what watercolorist would have dared use a palette knife on his paper? The knife is used today not only for applying paint, but for scraping out lights with its point; and its flat edge is used as a squeegee for pushing color around. I've also seen beautiful decorative flower pieces upon which paint rollers have been used to good effect.

This sort of unorthodoxy sets the purist's teeth on edge and sends him sulking to his ivory tower. Although I've said that a traditional transparent watercolor, well done by a painter who has something to say, can be a beautiful work of art, there's no reason why an artist should hold back if he has the urge to explore new methods.

I'm conservative by nature — or at least I think I am. I don't fling paint around recklessly, hoping that something will happen. When I start a painting, I know pretty well what I'm aiming for, even though I may stumble along the way and even end up by pulling the thing together in sheer desperation. If my picture has areas of opaque color, it's because I want opaque paint there, not because I tried to *salvage* what was intended to be a pure transparent treatment.

A few years ago, at an exhibition of watercolors by one of our finest workers in the medium, I saw a fellow artist examining one of the paintings with a magnifying glass. He turned to his companion and whispered the fatal word, "opaque." His day was complete. He'd found a bit of opaque in an otherwise transparent watercolor. That the picture might have been a work of art was secondary to *him*.

The point I want to make here is this . . .

There's no single *right* way to paint a watercolor. If you've found that the traditional method pleases you more than any other, then that is right for *you*. However, don't condemn the artist who departs from tradition. If you're a student, don't get stuck with one method. Experiment until you find yourself — find the way that's right for *you*.

Modern acrylics are quite finely ground. With a little practice, it's possible to obtain a very transparent wash. Good darks, however, require that you pick up plenty of paint if a really dark value is to be obtained at the first go. This is not so difficult when you're working directly on dry paper; but when a dark is put into a wet wash, it can spread and lighten unless the brush has been loaded with a generous amount of paint. A good example of combined opaque and transparent technique is the painting called *Cat in the Sun* on page 99.

The darkest tones in the upper right, above the rock wall, were obtained by using pure, undiluted pigment. This is true also of the dark green in the lower left corner. There's no transparency here. Both areas are quite opaque, yet the picture retains the freshness and luminosity we expect in a watercolor. I think this is due to the fact that no white paint was used anywhere and the handling is of the very direct virtuoso type we associate with the watercolors of John Singer Sargent.

If, instead of making use of the white paper for the light tones of the rock wall, I'd used white paint, the picture would have quite a different appearance.

I like the luminous transparency of sunlight and shadows playing on the rocks, as opposed to the opaque and semi-opaque darks of the trees and bushes. That's the effect I planned. It worked out. I was lucky.

Now let's see how white paint *can* be used to advantage without having the picture become opaque throughout. There's a method I've often used in watercolors and have since tried in acrylic with some interesting results. It's not to be confused with gouache. In gouache, the pigments are all mixed with white paint and are therefore all opaque. I have no name or label for this method. I'm sure I'm not the originator. I believe I've detected its use in studying the originals of some of the early masters of watercolor. Simply stated the method is this . . .

The paper is first covered with a thin application of white, to which a little yellow ochre has been added. This layer of color should be thin enough for any pencil drawing to show through; it merely serves to dampen the paper and leave a film of misty tone over the whole area. If the subject is a landscape, I start with the sky, allowing the wet undertone to blend with the color used for sky and cloud formations. By the time the sky has been completed, the film of white spread over the rest of the paper will be dry, or almost dry.

The rest of the procedure is the same as in working directly on dry paper, except that the color put down should be somewhat darker than usual as some of the underlying white will pick up. This is intended. It is the underlying veil of color, blending with the undercoat, that gives the picture painted in this manner an atmospheric quality difficult to achieve in any other way. Of course, it's easier to do this with regular watercolor than it is with acrylic, because watercolor dries more slowly. But it can be done with acrylic if the painter works rapidly.

It's an experiment to be tried. The worst that can happen is that a

Mabel, Minnie, and Maud Acrylic on watercolor paper, 14″ x 21″

There's an old stone bridge near where I live. I never passed it without thinking that there was a picture to be painted some day. It was so picturesque that I was afraid of it until, one day, I scrambled down the bank for a close look at the arch, and discovered the three ducks. I knew right then what I'd been doing wrong: I'd been considering the whole bridge, when actually the best approach was a closeup. I was lucky. The ducks swam around long enough for me to sketch them in with pencil; they were even there during most of the time I was painting. Except for some

opaque touches in the weeds and the small reflection below the nearest duck, this is a transparent rendering. I painted around the ducks, saving the white paper. The stonework of the bridge was first painted with warm tones of burnt umber and burnt sienna. Cool washes of phthalocyanine blue were painted over this; because the paint was acrylic, there was no pickup whatever. The sunlight, reflecting in the water and spotted on the banks, was left white paper, then washed over with pale color washes when the surrounding dark tones had dried.

The Wood Lot, Winter Acrylic on watercolor paper, 22″ x 30″

Here's one of the many paintings I've made of the woods behind the studio: a gray day picture without benefit of blue shadows on the snow! I like the dark shapes contrasting with the light tones of the snow. This was very simply painted, most of it with a flat 1″ brush. The distant tree mass was laid in with a large flat wash of gray, made with a mixture of burnt umber and phthalocyanine blue. When this was dry, the whole area was gone over with drybrush to create texture. This can best be seen below and at the sides of the patch of light sky. The light tree trunk at the right was left white, and then toned when the background around it had dried. The light parts of the snow are untouched white paper. The twiggy bushes, coming through the snow in the foreground and middle distance, are not exactly where nature planted them. I placed them where I thought they would do the design or composition the most good. The only opaque touches are the few dried beech leaves that remain on bush and branch. They were the last part of the picture to be painted.

piece of paper will be spoiled. It's only a piece of paper, but it's frightening, of course. Everyone working in the medium has experienced that fear. Spoil it if you must. Discard it and start again. Plenty of pictures have been ruined through *fear* of spoiling. I often tell students that nothing worthwhile was ever accomplished in watercolor with timidity.

Bubbles can produce texture.

Putting bubbles to work

When he first uses acrylic in the watercolor technique, the painter may be troubled by seeing bubbles appear as his brush sweeps over the paper. A quick brushstroke gets rid of them, or they will disappear without the painter having to do anything. However, this bubbling can also be used to some advantage in developing interesting textures. In painting rocks, I often make use of textures that (as far as I know) can be obtained only with acrylics. This is how it's done . . .

Let's suppose that the rock has been painted with its form clearly defined in three values: light, middle tone, and shadow. Now a flat brush is loaded with darker tone than the rock's middle tone, laid flat upon the rock, then lifted slowly off, leaving a texture made up mostly of bubbles. On drying, the bubbles leave a web-like texture that can be quite realistic. This method can also be used for rough tree bark or to suggest the nature of many rough surfaces. It's a trick; like all tricks, it shouldn't be overdone.

Fingernail scratches in wet paint.   Spatter.

Experimenting with textures

My advice is to experiment with your acrylics. Find out what they can or cannot do. It's possible to create a great many more textural effects with them than with traditional watercolor paint. Brush textures that would be difficult, even impossible, in any other medium can often be done easily with acrylic.

For instance, the artist's fingernails can be used to scratch patterns into wet opaque or semi-opaque paint. Here again, the fast drying acrylic calls for rapid work. I often use my fingernail for scratching in tree branches; or three or four fingers have been used at once to suggest weed patches. But another word of warning — don't overdo it.

Spatter work is a very old device for creating textures. It's usually done by dipping a watercolor brush in paint, holding it in a horizontal position over the paper, and tapping it on the handle of another brush or a pencil. How coarse or how fine will the spatter be? This depends on how far from the paper — or how close — the brush is held. Some artists prefer an old toothbrush. This is held in a vertical position and the blade of a palette knife is dragged over the bristles.

Heightening with white

In painting in a combination of opaque and transparent color, heightening with white is a method that can be used. Let me give you an example. Suppose the subject is a group of light colored flowers against a stone wall.

The wall, being stone, is heavily textured. To paint this texture carefully around each flower *might* be the correct approach if we were working in tempera. However our aim is to make a bold, free statement with a combination of opaque and transparent color. Obviously, the easiest way will be to paint the wall background first, then paint the flowers over it.

The flowers are sketched lightly with chalk on the dried background. Any unwanted chalk marks that remain on the completed picture can be removed with a soft cloth. Now, some of the flowers are quite brilliant in color, and some have delicate tints. Mixtures with opaque white would yield rather dull tones. So the flowers are painted with *pure white* over the stone wall background. Their shadowed areas can be painted simply with a light gray: perhaps a mixture of white with a touch of Mars black. This should be a halftone, never a dark tone. When the flowers have been painted (without details) in this manner, and are quite dry, you can paint or glaze thin, transparent washes of color over them. A few final touches of opaque are added to bring out the detail, and the flowers are finished. The darks of foliage and other details can be painted with opaque tones before, during, or after painting the flowers.

I shall have more to say concerning acrylic textures in the next chapter, where I deal with the tempera technique.

Cat in the Sun Acrylic on watercolor paper, 15″ x 22″

Miss Pepys, our cat, has appeared in many of my pictures, though I hadn't planned on her appearance in this one. I'd set up my gear one morning to try to capture the effect of sunlight and shadow on the old rock wall that runs along one side of the garden. I'd just roughly indicated the composition when Pepys came along the top of the wall and sat down. I was delighted. Knowing she might stalk off at any moment, I painted her in as rapidly as I could swing the brushes. The cat's portrait was finished before any-

thing else was painted. As the last brushstroke went in, she departed right on cue. This painting is a mixture of transparent and opaque. The dark tones in the upper right and lower left foreground were painted with pure, undiluted pigment and are quite opaque, while the sunlight and shadow tones of the rocks are transparent in treatment. I think the combination works in a free, loose approach like this. It's when they're combined in a *tight* rendering that I find the effect disturbing. Study the detail on the left.

Portal to the Past Acrylic on Masonite, 20″ x 19″

This is an early American house, abandoned and in ruins, a picture very carefully done in tempera technique. It was painted several years ago when I was more interested in this kind of approach than I am at present. I spent a great deal of time on it. The first step was a watercolor sketch, just to become familiar with the subject. Next, a detailed drybrush drawing was made with waterproof drawing ink. I diluted this with some water to make a dark gray, rather than jet black. An outline tracing was made from the drawing and traced onto the Masonite panel. The panel was

prepared with four coats of acrylic gesso, each one sanded smooth. The drawing was gone over with ink. For this, I used a No. 1 pointed sable watercolor brush. I put in some washes of burnt umber to set the composition and then started to develop the detail. Many seem to think the minute detail is the most interesting part of this picture. However, I know it's the abstract design or pattern that's the important thing here. Without it, the time spent on the detail would be wasted effort.

Chapter 8

Acrylic as tempera

The effects obtained with traditional egg tempera can be duplicated so easily with acrylic (see Demonstration 5) that I wonder why anyone would continue to use egg or emulsions of egg, oil, and water. I've tried both and if one of my early egg temperas is placed beside a more recent acrylic tempera, I must admit that they look alike to me.

Combining egg and acrylic

Some artists actually combine egg tempera and acrylics, claiming that this combination imparts a certain satin-like quality that we associate with egg tempera. This is how it's done. The yolk of the egg is separated from the white. This can be done by carefully pouring the egg back and forth between two glasses. The yolk is then broken into a container, covered with a lid, and stored in the refrigerator. It should last four or five days — longer, if it's kept cool when it's in the studio, but not in use.

Egg yolk is mixed with acrylic paints in the proportion of two parts yolk to three parts paint. No medium is used when you're painting. Water is used to thin the paint.

This is all very interesting — if you want to bother with it. I don't. I find that my "tempera" paintings in acrylic have the surface quality I like if I simply use the paint as described in this chapter.

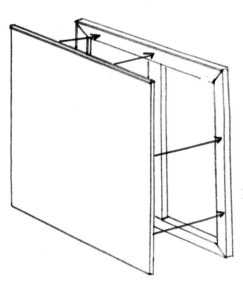

Panels larger than 16″ x 20″ should be fastened to a wooden frame or "cradle."

Support for acrylic "tempera"

A tempera painting should have a rigid support. Masonite is excellent for this purpose. The untempered kind should be purchased — see Chapter 2 — and its smooth side sandpapered lightly to create a bond between the surface and the gesso priming.

Panels larger than 16″ x 20″ should be fastened to a wooden frame.

This can be made of 1″ x 2″ pine, obtainable in any lumber yard. Here is a sketch of how the frame (or cradle, as it's called) looks before glueing the panel to it. For this, I use Elmer's glue, coating the wood and the Masonite panel where it will contact the wood. I put the frame, glue side up, on the floor and place the panel on it. This is weighted down with books (or anything else that's handy) and allowed to dry overnight.

Gesso ground

The next step is the gesso ground. The traditional gesso was always a nuisance to prepare from all those raw ingredients, cooked in a double boiler. The new acrylic gesso is a joy to use, coming in cans and ready to apply. For the first coat, I thin it a little with water. The other coats come straight out of the can. I find that three coats usually give me the surface I require.

If a very smooth surface is desired, each coat should be sandpapered with extra fine sandpaper on drying. Before applying the first coat, it's good practice to coat the *back* of the panel, including the wood frame, with a coat of gesso which can be thinned with water for this purpose. By doing this, we not only prevent warping, but also seal the panel.

Preliminary drawing

We now have a beautiful, gleaming white panel, ready to paint upon. First, however, comes the drawing. Tempera painting needs careful planning. This is no rapid virtuoso medium. I start by sketching my composition lightly with charcoal on the gesso ground. If figures are to be part of the subject, I draw them on tracing paper the size I want them, then trace them onto the gesso surface. To do this, I simply rub the back of the drawing with a soft pencil; fasten it in position on the panel with a little Scotch tape; and go over the drawing with a hard pencil — a 2H works well.

After removing the tracing paper, I go over my drawing with diluted Mars black, using a No. 0 pointed sable watercolor brush. As soon as this step is finished, I dust off the charcoal with a soft cloth and I'm ready for the color.

Painting method

My painting is started with thin color washes. At this stage, the painting looks like my usual transparent watercolors. When I think of all the work that lies ahead to make this a tempera painting, I confess that I'm sometimes tempted to leave well enough alone and quit right there.

When the panel has been completely covered with the thin washes, the gradual build-up of color begins. I usually develop one part at a time. This procedure is exactly opposite to the technique I use in oil or watercolor, where I work all over the picture, gradually bringing it to completion. If my subject is a landscape with a sky, I complete the sky, using soft hair watercolor brushes of the smaller sizes — Nos. 0, 2, and 1 being used most. Small brush strokes of warm and cool color tones overlap to create the smooth, but vibrant surface we associate with tempera painting.

Having completed the sky, I move on to another area. If the subject

The Clam Diggers Acrylic on Masonite, 16″ x 25″

Having grown up on a rocky coast, I find that rock forms fascinate me. Although I don't paint the typical dashing wave marine, I often find subjects along the shore. This group of rocks on Wingaersheek Beach, Massachusetts, has a very interesting variety of forms. I've painted them several times from different points of view. This version is the best to date. Actually, the rocks aren't quite as large as they appear here. By making the figures smaller than they really would be, I've changed the scale, and the rocks become massive. The picture also gains depth. By using a warm gray tonality, with some blue gray in the distant ocean and in the clothing of the figures, I tried to suggest the moisture laden atmosphere of a summer morning on the coast. The panel was given four coats of acrylic gesso. For the painting, I used only soft hair watercolor brushes. Much of the rock texture was obtained by laying a loaded brush flat on the rock surface, then lifting it off. This creates a mottled effect that I've been unable to duplicate in any other medium. Collection, Lezius Hiles Company, Cleveland, Ohio.

contains a house, I may decide to spend a few hours on it. Or there may be an interesting group of trees I'm itching to get to work on. The trick is to keep the overall tonal value relationship correct while finishing the picture piece by piece.

Piece by piece, the picture gets done, and finally there comes the day when I feel glad that I *didn't* stop when it was in the first stage.

Rendering minute detail will *not* suggest the illusion of reality if the value relationships aren't correct. That's why it's so important to establish good values with the thin watercolor lay-in before finishing any one part of the painting.

Brushes

In the completed painting, none of the early lay-in will be visible; it has all been covered by hundreds, even thousands, of small, opaque brushstrokes. I've painted some pictures (small ones) with only the three brushes previously mentioned.

However, for covering large areas, and for creating different textural effects such as foliage or dense weed patches, I use a greater variety of brushes. A large, old, well worn watercolor brush is a splendid tool. A round No. 9, worn short and square, can be used in many ways. It can be loaded with paint, flattened, and spread on the palette. Lightly dragged over the picture surface, it leaves thin lines. It can be stabbed straight at the panel to leave a pattern of spots. Cheap housepaint brushes can be cut and shaped by the artist for special purposes.

Other tools

One's manner of painting in tempera is a highly personal matter, as it should be. I think the artist should experiment with his brushes or with any other tool that will help him obtain the effect he desires.

In contemporary tempera paintings, many effects look as though they took hours of tedious labor to work out, but were actually done in a relatively short time with the help of some clever tool other than the conventional brush.

For instance, a Kleenex tissue, crumpled in the hand, dipped in paint, and touched to the surface of the panel, will leave a textural effect that would be difficult to execute with a brush. This texture can be used in many ways when painting landscapes or seascapes. Bits of rag, especially rough toweling, are also useful. I've even used steel wool, patting and dragging it along the picture surface. Sandpaper, rubbed over a dry area, will bring some of the light undercoat through; I've seen this used to suggest the sparkle of distant water.

Of course none of these tricks — for tricks they are — should be overdone. The major part of the work must be carried out with the brush, and a small brush at that.

The quiet, beautiful surface of a good tempera painting is — whether egg tempera or acrylic "tempera" — is painstakingly arrived at by a lot of careful brushwork. Whatever else was used to assist the artist (in building up textures or suggesting details) should *not* be evident.

Texture produced by crumpled Kleenex.

Rough toweling can produce texture, as can bits of rag.

Steel wool, patted and dragged over the surface, can produce surprising textures.

The exhibitions of the works of Andrew Wyeth, and the publicity given that fine American painter, have recently brought about a new interest in realism and the tempera technique. My advice to anyone who has the urge to try it is this: if you don't have the disciplined temperament for it, leave it alone. Ask yourself these questions and give yourself honest answers.

Question one: Can I draw realistically and well? If you want to paint a good realistic picture, you must be able to draw. There are many young artists today who *cannot.* They were never taught.

Question two: Am I willing to spend day after day, week after week, on the same picture? Do I have the patience for it?

Question three: Will I be able to keep from murdering the first friend who says, "Very nice, but why imitate Andrew Wyeth?"

If you still want to work in the tempera technique after reading the above, then go ahead. Maybe you *do* have the temperament.

I paint an acrylic "tempera" only when I feel a great need for a change of pace: for instance, when I've spent a whole summer painting watercolors that are done at top speed and take no more than an hour to complete. I don't think I have the real temperament for a tempera painter — not 100% anyway — because by the time I've finished a tempera painting, I'm never in the mood to start another, and a whole year may slip by before I again feel the urge. In the meantime, I go back to my oils, watercolors, or acrylics with a renewed interest in the freer, more spontaneous methods described in earlier chapters.

White Heather Acrylic on Masonite, 11³/₄″ x 18³/₄″

It's said that we Cornish are a superstitious lot. This is an exaggeration, of course. Nevertheless, it's true that finding white heather among the more common purple heather brings the finder good luck! This is a picture of the high moorland country between Penzance and St. Ives. Beyond the rocky outcropping is the ocean, unseen here, and beyond that is Ireland. The moors are colorful at all seasons. In the spring, the yellow gorse, and later the purple heather, mingling with ferns and bracken, make a colorful tapestry. This picture was carefully painted with soft watercolor brushes, mostly smaller sizes being used. The sky is a warm gray at the zenith, with a gradual change to a very pale gray at the horizon. The rocky headland is quite cool in color, as is the dark toned land leading out to it from the left. The large expanse of moorland from foreground to headland is in warm tones of ochre, burnt sienna, and dull green. The sweater on the figure is the darkest dark; for this, I actually used black! The only pure white in the picture is right where you'd expect it — the white heather in the hands of the model.

Edge of the Wood Acrylic on Masonite, 13″ x 19″

This study of ferns growing at the edge of the woods was painted throughout with soft hair brushes. This was because I wanted to experiment with acrylic glazes and at the same time keep the surface smooth. The brushes used were fairly well worn ox hair water-color brushes. The panel was given four coats of acrylic gesso. Each coat was sanded as it dried. I worked directly on the pure white gesso as I wanted it to shine through the transparent and semi-transparent layers of paint. Thin washes of warm and cool colors were first painted over the entire panel; I used burnt sienna, burnt umber, raw sienna, and phthalocyanine blue. This formed the background over which the ferns were painted. The ferns were all put in with a light toned mixture of white and AZO yellow. When dry, they were glazed with yellow green — mixtures of AZO yellow, raw sienna, and a touch of phthalocyanine blue — and a blue green obtained by mixing phthalocyanine blue and AZO yellow. Additional work was then done on the background to create textural interest. Drybrush was used and dark washes were painted swiftly over light areas and allowed to form bubbles. When acrylic bubbles break and dry, they create a unique pattern of spots. The picture is mostly warm in color as it was painted in late summer, when the ferns had lost their first fresh green. Study the detail of this painting on the right.

Toward Tintagel Acrylic on Masonite, 9¹/₂″ x 20″

Here's an outcropping of lichen covered rocks, over-looking a flat stretch of moorland, typical of many parts of Cornwall. The young woman is Gloria, wife of painter Tom Nicholas. Although this is a small paint-ing, I think it has a "big feel." This is partly due to the huge rocks contrasting with the figure, but also to the minute detail of the foreground, which is in contrast to the quiet, more simply painted middle distance. I think the composition works as I planned it. The eye goes first to the figure because of the head silhouetted against the luminous sky. Then, instead of following the rocks, I think the eye moves to the left along the light struck distant ocean and comes to rest at the group of . ees. Because the head is turned in that direction, this also helps move the eye along. The only really bright colors are the girl's cerulean blue sweater and a touch of red orange for a bit of the scarf show-ing over the shoulder. The foreground autumn grass is painted in green and ochre tones. The rocks range from warm gray to almost black. Collection, Adelphi College, New York. Study the detail of this painting on the left.

The Students Oil over acrylic on Masonite, 9″ x 12″

In the chapter on this technique, I've fully explained the procedure. It's a very old technique; most of the old masters used some kind of underpainting. In this little painting of some students watching their instructor painting, the underpainting is most easily seen in the background, above and behind the figures. Here the color is very thin, merely a rubbing of warm green; the brushwork and tonal variety of the underpainting show through. The bright lights of the clothing and the spots of sunlight are all opaque. The flesh tones of the girl in the large straw hat are thin glazes of warm color over the pale gray acrylic underpainting. Glazed paintings "eat up the light" and for that reason should be hung in a well lighted place.

Chapter 9

Acrylic as underpainting for oils

The old masters used tempera as an underpainting for oil. By first laying in the composition in tones of gray tempera, they shortened the process of painting to some extent. Most of the problems of drawing and composing were solved in the underpainting. Color was not considered until the monochromatic underpainting was completed.

An old master technique

This, in effect, is a division of the labor into two separate operations. It's still a good way to paint a certain kind of picture. Color glazes — over an underpainting of tones from medium gray to pure white — can produce colors almost jewel-like in quality.

Instead of tempera, we can use acrylic, which is ideal for underpainting (see Demonstration 6). In fact, I prefer it to the egg tempera which I previously used. Oil colors sit well on acrylics, and can also be wiped off (if necessary) without disturbing the underpainting.

The underpainting and glazing technique is best suited to figure compositions, portraits, still lifes, or nonobjective work. I don't recommend it for landscapes, which are best painted *alla prima,* which means "all at one go." Glazed landscapes don't have the atmospheric charm that's obtained by the direct, opaque painting we associate with the French Impressionists.

Underpainting

The acrylic underpainting should be done with few colors. I use only raw umber and white when I make an underpainting.

One should aim at a fairly light tonality; "pastel" probably describes it best. This light tonality is important because successive oil glazes darken the picture's tone. If the underpainting is too dark in value, the beauty of the color glazes — over cool, underlying grays — will be lost. For instance, think of the glaze as a sheet of colored cellophane. Place the sheet over a tone of very dark gray and the result is not exciting. However, lay a sheet of transparent blue or yellow cellophane over a light gray or near white tone, and the result can be compared to stained glass. That's what glazing is. Transparent color tones, with a properly prepared underpainting showing through, create an optical effect obtainable in no other way.

Details shouldn't be part of the underpainting, which should be free and loose in character. I try for a bold, simple statement, with the lightest areas white or a very light gray. All definite drawing comes *after* the color scheme has been well established. Only by working in this manner can you avoid a hard, tight rendering effect.

Return of the Native Acrylic on Masonite, 20″ x 24″

This old deserted home on the Boston Post Road was an interesting subject. Working on its tree sheltered, overgrown lawn was rather pleasant in the September sun. However, after many days on the spot, and many more in the studio, I was forced to conclude that perhaps I didn't have the tempera temperament after all. I haven't painted anything with so much detail since. A great amount of work went into this picture. The first version was a full sheet watercolor. Then I made a highly finished drybrush drawing. Before leaving the place, I shot some photographs of details such as the window, porch, etc. The picture, as you see it here, was painted in the studio with all my reference material pinned to the wall beside my easel. After laying in the composition with some bold washes over a careful pencil drawing, I painted the rest of the picture with my smallest watercolor brushes. It's a good portrait of the place, which was torn down the summer after this was painted. My method of working was to work on an area until I grew tired of it, then move to another part. Piece by piece, it developed and was finished at last.

114

A good underpainting should have body; that is, it should contain plenty of paint. Not all of the superimposed color tones will be pure, transparent glazes, but they *will* be relatively thin. Therefore, it's necessary to have good body in the underpainting, especially in the lights. Rough textures can be built up in some areas of the underpainting, while other parts may be left smooth. Interesting effects result when a rough texture is glazed and the glaze sinks into the depressions of the textured underpainting.

The pictures I've painted with glazes over acrylic underpaintings have all been done on Masonite panels, coated with acrylic gesso. Although I prefer to use only tones obtained with mixtures of raw umber and titanium white, colors *can* be used in the underpainting if you prefer.

Glazing

If you're new to this method, some experimenting should be done. Find out what happens when, for instance, a blue is glazed over yellow, or a red over green. The color effect you obtain will be quite different from the effect that results from mixing the colors on the palette. What happens is this: light *gleams through* the transparent glazes from the underpainting. On the contrary, when paints are mixed together on the palette and applied in an opaque manner, all the light is on the surface, not *within*.

To avoid a too glossy, mechanical finish, glazing shouldn't be overdone. Some covering or half covering tones, combined with glazes, are best. Glazing should be intelligently used as a tool or instrument, never as an end in itself.

In order to thin tube oil colors to the right consistency for glazing, a glaze medium is used. This can be purchased at the art supply store or prepared by the artist. I've found the copal painting medium manufactured by M. Grumbacher excellent for glazing. I mix a little of this medium with each mound of paint on the palette, and I also have some in a palette cup to dip into. There must also be turpentine to clean the brushes as the work proceeds.

There are many formulas for glaze mediums. Several reliable ones, quite simple to prepare, can be found in *The Artist's Handbook of Materials and Techniques* by Ralph Mayer and in *Formulas for Painters* by Robert Massey.

Glazes can be applied with brushes, rags, or the artist's thumb — which I seem to use more than the other two.

Well that's about it, except to remind you to keep that underpainting light in tone unless you want your picture to look like a dark hole in the wall.

Lanesville Cove, Cape Ann Acrylic on Upson board, 12″ x 16″

This picturesque cove, with its stone wharves, fishing boats, and houses clustered amid the trees surrounding the harbor, has been a favorite haunt of painters for a long time. I've painted it in all seasons and in all weathers. I never tire of Lanesville. It always has something to offer: low tide, when the flat rock ledges, forming the harbor floors, are exposed; the gulls resting on those rocks; the fog clothing everything in mystery. It's just great — that's all! This view is looking back from the harbor toward the road that comes down from the main highway. It was painted in early September while the trees were still in full leaf. The panel was prepared in advance with two coats of acrylic gesso and toned with a medium gray tone, consisting of a mixture of titanium white and burnt umber. First, I roughly blocked in the dark masses of the trees with a wash of burnt umber. Then came a few lines of the same color to indicate the buildings, road, stone wall in the left foreground, and the bow of the blue boat at the right. I then proceeded with the full color tones. As usual, the figures were put in last, placing them where I thought they would do the composition the most good.

116

Chapter 10

Classroom notes

What to paint? That's a question that seems to bother many students and amateurs. Actually, the world is full of things to paint. It's mostly a matter of learning to observe and to appreciate. It's also a matter of temperament. A Wyeth can see a subject in an old bucket on a post; but John Singer Sargent, on holiday from portrait commissions, painted watercolors from Venice to the Rocky Mountains.

The beginner often makes the mistake of looking for subjects in nature that remind him of pictures by a favorite artist. Too often, he passes up the thing that looked good, hoping that there will be something around the bend that looks just like a picture by so-and-so.

When you go outdoors to work, paint the first thing that interests you. If it was good enough to attract you in the first place, it's your subject. It's not what it is, but how you paint it that will make it interesting to the viewer.

If possible, join a class or a group that paints or sketches outdoors. You'll learn as much from your fellow students as you do from the instructor. And it's a great way to overcome that self-conscious feeling the beginner often has when he first experiences the thrill.of painting from nature.

Gray, overcast days are often more interesting to paint than the hard sharp contrasts of sunny days. Don't stay at home because the sun isn't out.

A clearing sky after rain is the landscape painter's delight.

When painting in the country, remember that someone owns the land. If possible, ask permission before trespassing. Pick up your used paint rags. This is a *must*. Don't make things difficult for the rest of us.

Fill a sketchbook with pencil sketches of trees drawn from nature. Learn the characteristics of the different types.

Paint your impression. Don't copy nature. When a bird flies through the air, you don't see the feathers.

You don't have to know as much about perspective as an architect to paint a landscape, but you should know the elementary principles . . . that is unless you're a primitive, and if you are, you shouldn't be reading this book.

When you submit paintings to a jury and get a rejection notice, don't be too upset. We've all had them. True, they're disappointing, but remember that a picture rejected by one jury could be (and often is) accepted by another. In forty years of exhibiting, I've never questioned the action of a jury — disagreed with them, yes, but privately, to myself.

When you receive a prize, don't let it go to your head. Only you and the awards jury think your picture worthy. Every other artist in the show is sure the prize should have been his.

There's a vitality in a sketch from nature that "afterwork" rarely has.

When I do a demonstration, people say, "You make it look so easy." Sure, but that's because it's a demonstration, a planned performance. They should see me at work in my studio or alone with nature — see me dig, groan, swear, scrape out, start over, hate myself, and feel awful!

You won't learn to paint *better* by using acrylics. You'll simply learn to use a new and different medium.

It's natural for art students to imitate the work of their instructor. But only the hacks *go on* doing it.

When you're working with acrylics, remember to keep your brushes wet.

Don't set your palette with as much acrylic color as you would when you're working with oils. Acrylics dry rapidly on the palette, as well as on the painting.

When painting anything, concentrate on tonal values first, and on color later.

Don't be afraid to spoil a paper or a canvas. You learn a lot while spoiling.

Use the biggest brush you can handle with comfort.

Avoid tightness; don't niggle. Try a little careful carelessness.

A studio should be a well organized workplace, clean and functional — like a barber shop. It shouldn't look like something out of a women's magazine. Nor should it look like a junk shop. Let's not be "arty."

If you see an artist at work outdoors, pass him by — he'll appreciate it. Besides, he's not a bit interested in your kid sister who can draw real good and never had a lesson in her life.

Twenty years ago, before I thought I was even middle aged, I was painting alongside New York's East river with a young student friend. Two tough looking teenage boys came along and stopped to watch my friend paint. They said nothing. After three or four minutes, one walked the hundred yards over to where I was working, looked at my painting, then turned and shouted to his buddy: "Hey Joe! Come on over here. The old guy's better!"

In the days of vaudeville, the entertainers had a motto or slogan: "Always leave them laughing when you say goodbye." With that in mind as I'm now about to take my leave, I hope I can at least raise a smile by reproducing my favorite picture of myself. Good luck and good painting.

Portrait of the author by Emery Clarke

The Wild Garden Acrylic on canvas, 30″ x 40″

Cinnamon fern and wild geranium grow in the wild garden along the edge of our wood lot. One of the joys of early spring is watching for the first bloodroot and hepatica to appear. I think a landscape painter has to be a nature lover, and I am. (I could never think of nature as H. L. Mencken did; he said, "Nature is a place to throw beer cans on Sunday.") I've painted this garden many times in all media: oil; water-color, transparent and opaque; now in acrylic. This is my largest effort to date. I stretched raw linen on the conventional canvas stretcher and coated it with four coats of acrylic gesso. I set up my easel in the garden among the ferns and started by rubbing in tones of mixed greens all over the canvas with a large house-paint brush. The mixtures were made of raw sienna, burnt sienna, and phthalocyanine blue. The canvas had been previously toned with a thin, transparent, warm tone of burnt sienna. Next came a few lines (a mixture of yellow ochre and white) to establish the composition. I worked for two hours at painting the detail. Then, because the light had changed, I carried the canvas into the studio, worked from memory for another hour, and called it done. The little geranium blossoms were first painted pure white; when dry, they were glazed with color. The next day, I varnished the picture with matte acrylic varnish. I look forward to more painting in the wild garden.

Demonstrations

Down East Step One

I first sketch in the composition with an HB pencil, using as few lines as possible. Notice how simply the forms are indicated, eliminating all detail.

Down East Step Two

Next, I mix a pale wash of burnt umber, using plenty of water, and I paint this over the entire picture surface to warm the cold white of the paper and make the surface more receptive to the washes of color that will follow. This first pale wash will also serve to provide the lightest tones of the picture, which are not absolutely white in this subtle, atmospheric treatment. The cool, middle tone of the clouds is put in — a mixture of the two colors, with more blue than umber to make the wash definitely cool.

Down East Step Three

I add the darker cloud shapes, using burnt umber with only a touch of blue this time. The brushwork is interesting here: I rapidly twisted and turned the brush to obtain a ragged, windblown quality. The main forms of the sky are now finished. I turned to other areas of the painting.

Down East Step Four

The distant land, wharf, and shore are put in with a wash of burnt umber. The forms are still flat and devoid of detail, which is saved for the last phase of the painting. At this point, the emphasis is still on the flat pattern. I attended to the details at a later stage of the painting.

Down East Step Five

Now the darks begin to appear, along with crisp accents, drybrush in the foreground to create the sparkle of the water, and carefully selected details like the figures on the wharf, boats and masts, birds, etc. The distance receives an overwash of cool color.

Down East Acrylic on watercolor paper, 11″ x 15″

In the finished painting, note the calligraphy of the foreground water and the middle tones of the wharf and the shore. The details that bring the painting to life — boats, birds, figures, the drying net hanging from the mast on the far side of the wharf—were saved for the very last. Painted with just two colors — burnt umber and phthalocyanine blue — the picture has a surprising range of color, demonstrating that just two hues can create the illusion of far more color than is actually used. Study the detail on the facing page.

Morning in Maine Step One

Most of my outdoor paintings are done without any preliminary pencil drawing. A few lines usually suffice to map out the composition. As a rule, these are done with some diluted burnt umber. However, when pencil *is* used, it's kept at a minimum and appears about as you see it here.

Morning in Maine Step Two

The dark greens of the distant land and the dark reflections in the water are the first color washes painted. The lower edge of the reflection is wetted with clean water to create a soft blend. Colors used are yellow ochre, raw sienna, phthalocyanine blue. A pale wash of yellow ochre is painted over the light part of the water and a horizontal band of cool gray (phthalocyanine blue and burnt umber mixed) is painted into it wet in wet. This tone can be seen just above the boat. The foreground weeds and grass are given a wash of yellow ochre, mixed with a little burnt sienna.

Morning in Maine Step Three

The distant land and reflections are now strengthened with the same colors as before. The dory and its reflection in the water are painted with a warm wash of burnt sienna. The lobster traps are indicated by putting down their middle tones with a mixture of phthalocyanine blue and burnt umber. More burnt sienna brushwork is added to the foreground. Some drybrush work suggests sparkle on the water.

Morning in Maine Step Four

The picture is almost finished in this step. The deep darks in the right middle distance are added with burnt umber and more drybush. When this is dry, a wash of burnt sienna is painted over the drybrush. A cool wash of phthalocyanine blue is now painted over the dory and its reflection. Details like the red stripe at the water line, mooring lines, etc., go in. A few dark flecks on the water represent floating weed. I in-dicate the construction of the lobster traps with a dark mixture of burnt umber and phthalocyanine blue. More reddish brown darks go into the foreground (burnt umber, burnt sienna, and raw sienna) and some lights are quickly scratched out with a fingernail. When this area was quite dry, I dragged a 1″ flat brush, dipped in burnt umber, over it to create tex-tural interest in that passage.

Demonstration 2: transparent technique   **133**

Morning in Maine Acrylic on watercolor paper, 20″ x 28″

This is one of the many tidal creeks I explored during a two week trip to Maine in October. I was attracted to this spot by the contrast of the water, reflecting a pale sky; the darks of the distant shore; and the rich textures and color of the foreground. The dory and lobster traps were observed next and the whole thing wrapped itself up in my mind. One should see the big things first: the big, over-all effect; the lighting; the tonal values; the shapes. You must not, on seeing a dory, think that you must paint a picture with a dory

because you've seen one by Wyeth or someone else. Don't search for subject matter that reminds you of your favorite painter. Paint something that has attracted *you*. I think the contrast of the quiet water and the busy textures of the foreground are interesting. Notice the light streaks in the grass and weeds. These were lifted out of the wet paint with the back of my fingernail, using a swift, upward stroke. Study the detail on the left.

November on the Saugatuck Step One

The first step is an important one because the composition is established at this initial stage. In a picture that's painted opaquely, compositional changes can be made as the work proceeds, but it's always best to design the space well at the start. As a rule, I first decide where my horizon will be and indicate it with a line. In this sketch it's just below the center of the space. (I felt that the buildings and tall tree breaking the skyline would compensate for the horizon being so close to the center.) With a little burnt umber, fairly well diluted with water, I begin by sketching the composition as shown here. My plan is to have the eye enter the picture by way of the water in the foreground, and be guided to the house, which I wanted to be the dominant point of interest. I now paint the sky, using yellow ochre, burnt umber, and cerulean blue, with titanium white, loosely mixed to obtain the effect of sun shining through thin, moist clouds.

November on the Saugatuck Step Two

The land areas are now put in with broad, flat tones. The distance is painted with a warm gray mixture of burnt umber and white, then some cool gray (cerulean blue, burnt umber, and white) rapidly painted into it. The land area to the left and the marsh grass to the right are painted with warm colors; the autumn frosts had caused them to change from green to tones of ochre and sienna. Here I use yellow ochre, raw sienna, burnt sienna, and white. The light tone of the water is put in with the same colors that I used in the sky. Up to this point, there's been no attempt to define details and the houses are still untouched.

November on the Saugatuck Step Three

In this stage, I begin searching for significant details that will suggest — merely suggest — reality. I start by painting in the buildings and the tall tree. The house is put in flatly, using burnt sienna toned down with a little burnt umber. Getting the correct tonal value is important here. The foliage of the tree is painted with raw sienna. The pattern of rocks and reflections in the water are next. Now some dark tones are added to the buildings and some scumbles of the same on tree and river banks. The final details, painted with a small pointed watercolor brush, are a suggestion of bullrushes in the right foreground, some tall utility poles in the distance, and the tree trunk; these will be seen in the color reproduction.

November on the Saugatuck Acrylic on Upson board, 8″ x 11″

Although this is one of my smallest paintings, it's a favorite of mine. It was painted at Wild Duck Haven on the Saugatuck River in Westport, Connecticut. Some unexpected warm weather, a couple of days after Thanksgiving, provided the opportunity to paint outdoors. This scene, which I'd been observing for some time, is good for most of the year, but especially good in late fall, when the salt hay of the marsh has turned color and some leaves are off the trees. The reason for its small size was the fact that I'd picked up a nice little frame in a second hand shop and cut a panel to fit it. Like most of my small sketches, it was rapidly painted in order to catch the early morning lighting effect. I think it's a good example of an impression without detail, depending on the tonal value relationship for its illusion of reality. A few sketchy lines of burnt umber served to indicate the composition, then, as almost always, I started with the sky. The warm and cool grays of the distance were obtained with cerulean blue, burnt umber, and white, loosely mixed. The land areas to the left and right were the next to go in; the house, tall tree, and the foreground rocks were last. A few dark accents, suggesting details, were actually the finishing touches.

November on the Saugatuck Detail of Step Three

Compare this with the detail of Step Four on the facing page.

November on the Saugatuck Detail of Step Four

The Wood Lot Step One

I always start a wood interior by establishing an abstract pattern of light and dark. The details — tree trunks, branches, and twigs — aren't considered until the picture is well on the way. The student or beginner gets bogged down in a mess of detail much too soon. Sunlight and shadow in the woods are complex and confusing; the effect changes rapidly. To change with it as you paint is to end in frustration. It's therefore necessary to seize a definite lighting effect at the start and stay with it. This illustration shows how I rapidly put down the pattern I want to hold at the finish, no matter how much detail I may add later. The light area is a pale wash of AZO yellow medium, and the darker tone is a green obtained with a mixture of AZO yellow medium and a touch of phthalocyanine blue.

The Wood Lot Step Two

Now I strengthen the pattern. A variety of greens are used in the top half, all made with mixtures of AZO yellow medium, raw sienna, and phthalocyanine blue.

I used a 1½″ flat nylon brush here. Some drybrush is visible. The value of the foreground is also darkened somewhat.

The Wood Lot Step Three

Now, for the first time, some opaque color is used, scattered around to indicate leaves catching the light, both on the trees and on the ground. The brightest spots are put in with pure titanium white to be glazed with color later. The other leafy indications are green mixtures of yellow, blue, and white. Some deeper greens, obtained with a mixture of raw sienna and Mars black, go into the foreground, middle distance, and upper foliage areas. In the next stage, I attended to other areas.

The Wood Lot Step Four

The picture is now ready for tree trunks and other details. These aren't necessarily placed where they occur in nature, but placed with the design of the picture in mind. The opaque spots are now glazed with color washes: the bright ones with a transparent wash of AZO yellow; the others with various green mixtures. As most of the trunks are seen against the light, a fairly dark mixture of burnt umber and Mars black is used. These darks are quite opaque. With a few final opaque light spots, the picture is finished.

The Wood Lot Acrylic on watercolor paper, 20″ x 28″

The constantly changing pattern I see from behind the studio is different at each season, but always beautiful. This painting was made outdoors in June. It's a combination of transparent and opaque techniques. I always start a wood interior by making a kind of abstract of the big light and dark shapes. Not individual trunks or branches — they come later. Once the pattern has been established, it's best to hang onto it because, like the clouds, it won't stand still. Here my main light is in the picture's center, with the foreground in shadow. Before I'd finished the lighting was quite different. This type of painting is best done rapidly; although it's painted on the spot, much must be done from memory. Capture that first impression, don't count leaves, and remember that the birds can fly through the woods. In my demonstration, I've tried to show the steps taken in painting a wood interior of this kind: first the abstract pattern; then the tree trunks; and finally the few details that create the illusion of reality. Study the detail on the left.

The Old Burroughs Place Step One

On the pure white gesso panel, I draw the subject in pencil. This is merely an outline drawing; no attempt is made to put in any details. I'm concerned only with composition: the designing of the picture space; the arrangement of the major elements within the four borders of the panel. When the pencil outline is completed, I put in a few simple color washes. Notice that much of the space has been left white.

The Old Burroughs Place Step Two

This illustration shows that I've started building up the foreground. However, these are still transparent color washes, painted as I would develop a traditional watercolor. The only opaque areas are the sky and the distant mountains, neither of which is finished. The sky will have to be gone over three or four times to create the opaque but vibrant atmospheric quality I desire. Colors used in the sky are yellow ochre, burnt umber, and Mars black in mixtures with titanium white. Colors used in the foreground are yellow ochre, raw sienna, burnt sienna, burnt umber, and titanium white, plus some dull greens obtained by mixing raw sienna and Mars black.

The Old Burroughs Place Step Three

Now the fun begins. Here's where I start to develop a piece here, a piece there. I first give the sky its second coat, just to build up the paint thickness. Then, with a couple of pointed watercolor brushes, I go to work on the dark pine trees, using mixtures of raw sienna, phthalocyanine blue, and Mars black. When they reach the stage you see here, I move on to the house and establish a few of its darker values to obtain the correct relationship with the sky. That foreground full of weeds is calling, so I quit the house and have a grand time building up all kinds of tex-

tures, using crumpled Kleenex, old worn watercolor brushes, spatter, and drybrush. This is all opaque. The gesso has been completely covered on this right side, while the left side remains as it was in Step Two. The color reproduction shows how much more work is done to finish the picture. This type of painting requires a slow, careful buildup, often covering up today what took an hour or two to do yesterday. That's why I say: if you don't have the temperament for the tempera technique, don't do it!

The Old Burroughs Place Acrylic on Masonite, 24″ x 42″

The Pellews spent many happy vacations on this farm, which nestles on the slopes of North Twin Mountain in New Hampshire. It was quite a shock to return, after a twenty year absence, to find it abandoned and its lawns and fields gone to weeds. We just walked around the house and "remembered when": evenings spent around the wood stove in the kitchen, swapping yarns with Jud Burroughs; pitching horseshoes in the evening after a day of painting or climbing the trails; going for the milk; walking our little daughter to the village store for ice cream; remembering dozens of things we shall never do again. A sad day. I made a drybrush drawing and took some photographs. The picture (in tempera technique) was painted in the studio six months later when I'd recovered from the mood of that October day when we returned to Twin Mountain. Of all the pictures I've painted of New Hampshire, I like this one best. Could it be for sentimental reasons? I wonder.

Flowers in a Watering Can Step One

Canvas is prepared with acrylic gesso. The composition is sketched directly with the brush, using some burnt umber thinned with water. There's no attempt to draw individual flower petals or details of any kind.

Flowers in a Watering Can Step Two

This is the complete acrylic underpainting, painted throughout with burnt umber and white. The important thing here is to avoid the temptation to put in any dark tones. Remember: each time a tone is glazed with oil paint, that tone becomes darker in value. Dark tones and details do not belong in a well painted underpainting. The flowers at this stage are painted pure white. The light and shade of the watering can are simply stated. This step must be rich in pigment; plenty of paint should be used. It must be opaque throughout, containing no transparent washes. Note that some parts are left unfinished for demonstration purposes, to better describe the procedure.

Flowers in a Watering Can Step Three

In the upper left hand corner, the untouched acrylic underpainting is seen. The darkened band below it is a warm tone of burnt sienna oil paint, thinned with copal painting medium and turpentine. I spread it over the entire picture surface with my thumb and fingers. It serves to isolate the acrylic underpainting and to make the canvas more receptive to the oil paint that follows. This first application of oil color must be thin — transparent enough to allow the underpainting to show through. The major part of the illustration shows the background, developed with warm color glazes and some semi-opaque darks; burnt sienna and burnt umber are used. Color glazes are rubbed onto the flowers with the fingers and opaque brushwork is added to suggest petals and light and shade. The watering can, and the log on which it stands, are developed in the same manner: transparent tones are rubbed on and opaque brushwork defines the detail. This illustration shows the painting nearing completion. The final result is seen in the color reproduction.

Flowers in a Watering Can Oil over acrylic on canvas, 25″ x 30″

Like most artists, I like the informal bouquet. I detest formal "flower arrangements" as they're called. The tricks that florists and well meaning garden club people do with flowers leave me cold. These asters were picked in early autumn, put into an old watering can, and posed outdoors against a stone wall. I made no attempt to paint the individual stones of the wall because this would create competition for the flowers which, after all, were the subject of my picture. It was Robert Henri who said that a background should be painted as you see it when looking at your subject. It should *not* be considered separately. Good advice. I think composition is as important in a flower painting as in any other subject. Most amateurs place the bouquet in the exact center and make it too large or too small for the picture space. Note here how the watering can has been positioned off center, giving careful consideration to the placing of the flowers so there's no feeling of unbalance.

Index